Wimpy Parents

From Toddler to Teen–
How NOT
to Raise
a Brat

by

Kenneth Condrell, Ph.D., Child Psychologist,

with

Linda Lee Small

WARNER BOOKS

A Time Warner Company

Copyright © 1998 by Kenneth N. Condrell, Ph.D., and Linda Lee Small
All rights reserved.

Warner Books, Inc., 1271 Avenue of the Americas, New York, NY 10020

Visit our Web site at http://warnerbooks.com

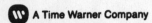 A Time Warner Company

Printed in the United States of America
First Printing: June 1998
10 9 8 7 6 5 4 3 2

Library of Congress Cataloging-in-Publication Data

Condrell, Kenneth N.
    Wimpy parents : from toddler to teen : how not to raise a brat / Kenneth Condrell, with Linda Lee Small.
        p.   cm.
    Includes index.
    ISBN 0-446-67367-6
    1. Parenting. 2. Child rearing. 3. Discipline of children.
4. Problem children. I. Small, Linda Lee. II. Title.
HQ755.8.C654 1998
649'.1—dc21   97-39547
                                                 CIP

Interior design by Charles Sutherland
Cover design by Elaine Groh
Cover illustration by Bonnie Timmons

YOU'VE TRIED THE WIMPY WAY....
NOW TRY A BETTER WAY...

AT BEDTIME

THE WIMPY WAY: When your two-year-old resists bedtime, you let him stay up and even take him to bed with you.

A BETTER WAY: You set a definite bedtime and make it a pleasant routine. You then place your toddler in his own bed and ride out any fussing with brief, reassuring visits. You are always careful not to turn your visits into a time of games and snacks.

AT DINNERTIME

THE WIMPY WAY: Almost every evening your eight-year-old gags at the sight of what you have prepared for dinner. You beg, scold, and threaten, then finally make him his favorite grilled cheese sandwich.

A BETTER WAY: A couple of times a week you cook your child's favorite dinner. In between these special days it is up to him to eat or not. When a timer goes off after twenty minutes, mealtime is over until breakfast.

WITH AN UNCOOPERATIVE CHILD

THE WIMPY WAY: Your twelve-year-old demands whatever he wants but becomes indignant when you want something from him. You yell, scream, and finally do the chores yourself—and still give in to his demands.

A BETTER WAY: You inform your twelve-year-old that life is a two-way street and stop all favors for a week. After he starts helping out, you respond to his requests.

"American parents need this challenge to be loving and consistent in a time of violence and boundary infringement. Condrell and Small's contribution is a must-read. It will benefit parents and children of all ages, guiding them in practical steps with loving humor and wisdom."

—Dr. Judith Landau, University of Rochester,
Division of Family Programs

This book is dedicated to my grandparents, Louie and Evdoxia Liakeas, who gave me an extraordinary childhood filled with love and adventure.

Acknowledgments

For many years, this book has been in my head but it was Agnes Birnbaum of Bleecker Street Associates who made it happen when she enthusiastically brought my ideas to the attention of Warner Books.

Communicating on paper what you have learned and what you believe in can be an incredibly challenging experience. Fortunately I had the good luck and pleasure of working with a terrific writer, Linda Lee Small. Her expertise with words and her sensitivity as a parent plus her bright, positive nature made the writing of this book a great experience.

Special thanks go to Colleen Kapklein. Colleen was always available for helpful discussions and kept all of us on schedule. I also want to thank Adaya Henis, Mari C. Okuda, and the entire staff of Warner Books for their efforts in making *Wimpy Parents* a reality.

CONTENTS

Section I: *What Is Wimpy Parenting?*   1
Introduction   3

CHAPTER 1
How to Tell if You Are a Wimpy Parent   8

CHAPTER 2
The Wimpy Parent Epidemic   17

CHAPTER 3
How Not to Raise a Brat   25

CHAPTER 4
The Secrets to Raising Successful Children   34

CHAPTER 5
Raising Moral Children in Today's World   46

Section II: *Taking Charge*   57
Introduction   59

CHAPTER 6
How to Be an Effective Parent   61

CHAPTER 7
How to Set Limits   70

CHAPTER 8
Rewards and Appropriate Punishment   86

CHAPTER 9
Creating a Wimp-Free Environment   98

Section III: *From Toddlers to Teenagers*   107
   Introduction   109

CHAPTER 10
   How to Survive and Enjoy Toddlers   111

CHAPTER 11
   Staying in Charge of Your Teen   124

Section IV: *Dealing with Pesty Behavior*   141
   Introduction   143

CHAPTER 12
   Sibling Rivalry   145

CHAPTER 13
   Taking Charge of Bedtime   156

CHAPTER 14
   Talking Back   166

CHAPTER 15
   Children Who Manipulate, Whine, and Lie   173

CHAPTER 16
   Picky Eaters   178

CHAPTER 17
   Morning Procrastinators   181

CHAPTER 18
   School Problems   185

   A Final Word   191

   About the Authors   193

SECTION I

—◦◦◦—

What Is Wimpy Parenting?

INTRODUCTION

Over the years, as a practicing family therapist and child psychologist, I have found myself spending more and more time counseling parents whose children were running them. In the 1980s I began to use the phrase "wimpy parenting" to refer to this parenting style. When I gave parent talks, audiences laughed when they first heard this expression. I would explain that wimpy parents are really nice people. I began to talk about the wimpy parent syndrome: There seemed to be an epidemic of parents who had lost control over their children. I began to see more clearly how parents were getting themselves into the trap of wimpy parenting, and finally I was developing strategies to help parents reclaim their rightful authority to be the leader, the boss, of their family.

What impressed me about the wimpy parent syndrome was that wimpy parents were often incredibly competent people. I recall saying to one father, "You are a veteran of the Vietnam

War, and yet you let your four-year-old walk all over you." That got his attention.

I also vividly recall a single-parent mom who was the host of a popular TV program. Professionally she was at the top of her game, but as a mom she was a wimp. In fact, she was ready to call off her forthcoming marriage when I first met her. Despite the fact that she had found the man of her dreams, she actually considered breaking her engagement because her four-year-old cried and said, "Mommy, I don't want you to get married." Mom was worried that forcing a stepfather on her child would really hurt her. I explained that most children who had lived for a long time alone with their mom would not like the idea of sharing her with another person. More importantly, I noted, she would be doing a good thing for her daughter by providing her with a two-parent home, since the child's father had disappeared long ago.

Fired up by my advice, this mom agreed to have a family counseling session that included her fiancé and her daughter. During this session the mom and her fiancé did what I had coached them to do: They lovingly but firmly told the girl, "We love each other very much, and we are going to get married and be a family. We also love you, and we are going to make sure you have plenty of time with each of us." Within a week this little girl had adjusted to the idea of Mom getting married, because Mom stopped being wimpy and didn't give in to an unreasonable request.

Wimpy parents are loving, well-intentioned parents who continually struggle to get their children to listen to them. They are dedicated parents and will, in fact, knock themselves out for their children. They expect their children to appreciate their efforts but find that their children give them a hard time: Instead of cooperating, their children confront them with arguments. Instead of respecting a no, their children continue to do what they have been told not to. Instead of being satisfied and grateful for all the special services and goodies they have received, these children demand more of everything.

Parents who have fallen into the wimpy parent trap express disbelief and confusion. They never would have dared to treat their own parents the way they are being treated. Many wimpy parents see themselves as much more involved with their children than their parents were with them. It seems only logical that their own children should be falling over themselves to please them instead of being so difficult.

In the last twenty years I have seen a steady increase in the number of parents falling into the wimpy parent trap. Particularly within the last few years, the problem has become so commonplace that I spend most of my professional time putting parents back in charge of their children. I'm helping some parents to be in charge of their children for the first time.

I was educated as a child psychologist in the 1960s. In the 1970s and 1980s I parented my own children. Now in the 1990s I watch too many children talk back to their parents, call them names like "butt head," use four-letter words without a sense of wrongdoing, refuse to help out at home or to do their homework, and argue with their teachers when they are corrected. Is it any wonder that in recent surveys more and more parents are claiming they would not choose to be parents if they had to do it over again?

Parenting styles and educational practices have gone through tremendous change. Experts promised parents that their new ideas would result in more self-confident and better-educated children. But all this change and experimentation has resulted in more brats, more frustrated parents, more poor students, and more unhappy teachers.

Wimpy Parents is a modern book rooted in the belief that today's good parenting should rely on yesterday's respect for authority.

Why This Book?

Children need their parents to be in charge, to coach and prepare them for life. To accomplish this, parents must be regarded by their children as the boss. *Wimpy Parents* teaches parents how to get their children to listen and to respect their authority.

Every parent has the potential to be a wimp—out of guilt, fatigue, and self-doubt. In today's psychological climate, divorced parents, remarried parents, single parents, married parents who both work, and parents of only children all easily stumble into the wimpy parent trap. That's a lot of potential wimpy parents!

Children never seem to run out of ways of behaving that leave their parents wondering, "Okay, what do I do now?" This book tells you just what to do now. When parents know how to handle their children's difficult behavior, their confidence goes zooming up. It's natural to feel positive when you have solved a problem.

In all my years of experience—in clinical practice, and dealing with the larger public as a speaker on radio and TV—I have found that there is a basic set of problems almost all parents face.

- How do you keep a two-year-old in her own bed?
- How do you handle a child who talks back?

- What do you do when your child creates scenes in public?
- What do you do when your child screams, "You're not fair!"?
- What do you do with a child who lies?
- How do you get siblings to stop fighting?
- How do you handle a teen who refuses to do homework?
- How do you handle a child who won't cooperate with his teacher?
- How do you get your children to help around the house?
- What do you do if you don't like your teen's friends?

Parents need answers, and this book provides them.

CHAPTER 1

———⟋⟋⟋———

How to Tell if You Are a Wimpy Parent

I can hear you saying, "I do things for my child all the time because I love him and want him to be happy. Does that mean I am a wimpy parent?" Loving and even occasionally giving in to your children is not synonymous with being wimpy.

Let's consider two scenarios.

Scene I: I was attending a wedding rehearsal party in the private home of the bride-to-be. Laid out in the dining room was one of the most lavish buffets I had ever seen. As relatives and friends lined up around the table, easily sixteen feet long, there was a knock at the door. The host answered only to find a delivery man with a large pizza. She was confused until a guest stepped forward. This woman, a mom with four children, admitted, "Oh, I ordered the pizza because that's all my kids like to eat." The other guests were astonished at the steps this mother had taken to accommodate her children. There was certainly enough food for her children to have chosen from.

Scene II: It was Halloween, and Jesse, age nine, suddenly developed strep throat. He begged his mom to let him trick or treat anyway, "I've started to take my medicine, and I won't breathe on anyone, honest." As his mother says, "Halloween is Jesse's favorite day—the only time he is allowed to be 'gross and yucky.' " A wimpy parent would have bundled him up and taken him out—with fingers crossed, hoping that he didn't make anyone else sick. But Jesse's mom held her ground. They dressed up in costumes, and Mom, wearing a red cape and horns, gave Jesse some of the candy meant for trick-or-treaters. But Jesse did stay in that night, to keep himself and other kids healthy.

This "devil mom" was acting out of love, not out of wimpy-ness. She doesn't routinely indulge all of her son's requests. On the other hand, the "pizza mom"—who never leaves home without the phone number for Domino's—is known by her neighbors to be exhausted by the demands of her children.

These characteristics clearly mark whether or not you are a wimpy parent:

- **Wimpy parents have a hard time being boss.** They often express their authority in a manner and tone that is just not convincing to a child. They are at a loss as to how to respond to their child's difficult behavior. Wimpy parents are often slow to recognize how their child's poor behavior has a negative impact on other people.
- **Wimpy parents give in too much.** Not recognizing that parenting is not a popularity contest, they hate to think

their child might not like them. Wimpy parents have a difficult time accepting and tolerating their child's anger or rejection. In an effort to avoid confrontations, they will do almost anything to keep peace and harmony. They give in to their child's behavior because they are too tired to deal with it or because they just don't know what to do about it.

- **Wimpy parents talk too much.** Wimpy parents have a strong need to be fair and logical, so they go into long, rational, persuasive discussions about why their child should comply with them. Their words often fall on deaf little ears; children like the opportunity to debate as if they are an equal. (When one parent gave up arguing and told her ten-year-old to just "please stop talking," the child responded with a discourse on her First Amendment rights to free speech.)

- **Wimpy parents are too patient.** Patience is, of course, a virtue. But the overpatient parent allows a child's inappropriate behavior to go on and on until the child has either gotten his own way or has received an extraordinary amount of parental attention for being negative. ("Now, honey, you know Daddy is on the phone, and I told you not to keep talking to me" is repeated over and over.)

- **Wimpy parents are inconsistent.** They stop their child from misbehaving one minute, and then the next instant they overlook the very behavior they just disapproved of. ("It's late, and she's too tired to clean her room." "We're at Grandma's house; let's not ruin it by sticking to rules.")

- **Wimpy parents take too much abuse.** Oftentimes wimpy parents are like magnets for abuse from their children. ("He doesn't really mean it when he calls me that name.") I've seen children actually biting or hitting their parents. ("Oh, she only hits me if I'm talking to someone," explained one woman, as if that explanation actually made sense.) They seem to be able to tolerate an excessive amount of obnoxious behavior.

- **Wimpy parents "save" their children from consequences.** They practically do their children's homework, will always make an extra trip to school with the forgotten lunch or gym outfit, and even write phony excuses. They smooth over all the rough edges of life.

- The bottom line is: **Wimpy parents love too much.** They believe that loving and nurturing a child is enough to promote good character and cooperation. They feel sorry for their children and don't want to make them unhappy by saying no. But this is certainly not good preparation for life in the real world.

What Wimpy Parenting Looks Like

One summer afternoon, I flew my small plane into a little airport in upstate New York. I walked across the street to a McDonald's restaurant. As I sat down, a flying buddy of mine walked in and joined me. Within a few minutes a five-year-old boy jumped up on the table right next to us and started pretending it was a trampoline. My friend turned to the boy and said, "Tables are not for dancing on." Without missing a jump, the boy shot back, "You're a stranger— strangers are not supposed to talk to little boys." The rude answer came back so fast it was amazing. This kid did not hesitate for a millisecond to challenge two adult men. He had almost learned the lesson about not talking to strangers, but he had no respect for adult authority. We decided to ignore him. Unfortunately, his brother joined him, and together they did their trampoline act on the table next to us. Suddenly their mother screamed, "Get over here!" That is all she ever said.

This story illustrates key characteristics of wimpy parenting. First, when misbehavior is allowed to continue, the child enjoys what he is doing and is "encouraged" to do it again. It is very important to put an end to inappropriate behavior as fast as possible. Second, it is not enough to tell a misbehaving child to "Get over here." Young children need to know why they were out of line and that their behavior was offending others. If they don't know that they did something wrong, they need to be made to feel guilty. For example, a parent might say, with a tone of disbelief, "Do you have any idea how you were bothering those nice men over there? I'm disappointed with your behavior." The parent could follow up by saying, "We are going over there, and you are going to apologize for bothering them." (For more strategies, see Section III.)

Wimpy parents do none of this. Instead they allow the children to bother others and be a nuisance way too long. The wimpy parent who does finally intervene fails to provide a specific lesson for the child. The child receives no feedback on what he has done or how the parent disapproves of such behavior.

Consistent Discipline Is Key

One morning I walked into a waiting room of a clinic to get a cup of coffee. There was a little girl in the waiting room with a woman who appeared to be her mom. As I poured coffee, the little girl shouted at me, "What are you doing here?" Before I had a chance to respond she added, "Get out of here, now." Her mother looked up from her magazine and said, "Hey." The only correction this little girl received for being disrespectful was one "Hey."

Wimpy parents allow their children to get away with misbehavior and do not take the time to inform their children of what they did wrong and what is the right way to behave. When a little girl can rudely challenge an adult man she has never seen before, you know she has had plenty of practice running the adults in her life.

Making Excuses for a Bully

A mom came to see me because her kindergarten-age son was aggressive and hit other children in school. The school had advised the mother to get counseling for her son. I asked her what she had done when she first learned that her son was bullying other children. Her answer was that she had gone to an allergist (!) and asked the doctor to take air samples at the kindergarten. This mom was convinced that her son's nasty behavior resulted from an allergy, and she managed to find a doctor who agreed with her. I was introduced to a little bully who was taking allergy pills.

One day, after I had been talking to the mom alone, we discovered that her son was not in the waiting room. He was in the parking lot. The mom's response to this potentially dangerous situation was, "Oh, that Jimmy." Jimmy was never informed that leaving the office without permission was wrong. In fact, Jimmy never heard that bullying other children was wrong. Jimmy was never held responsible for his behavior. (He simply had an allergy.) Wimpy parents often find excuses for their children's poor behavior, which lets the children off the hook. Jimmy never got much better, and he went on to be a bullying high school student—who *still* took allergy pills.

Golden rule:
Your children can't always be happy.

It's unrealistic to expect your children to be happy all the time. A parent who lives by the principle that all she wants is for her children to be happy will be marching ahead of them, trying to neutralize life and arrange it so they will avoid all problems. This approach robs your children of the chance to exercise their own personalities. Let them experience their happy and sad times.

The Wimpy Parent Test

Take this test to see if *you* qualify as a wimpy parent.

- Do you feel like your child is running you?
- Does your child talk back to you, speak disrespectfully, and call you names?
- Does your child rarely take no for an answer and hardly ever cooperate with requests?

- Do you feel like you have to bend over backward to be a good parent?
- Do you find yourself frequently "helping" your child with homework or getting him out of jams?
- Does the thought of making your child unhappy cause you to hold back from disciplinary measures?
- Do you feel guilty that you do not have as much time for your child as you want to?
- Are you reluctant to spoil what little time you have with your child by upsetting her with discipline?
- Do you have to ask your child ten times to do something and then raise your voice and threaten him to finally get cooperation?
- Do you find that no matter how much you do for your child she wants more and more?
- Does it break your heart to see him upset when you set limits and have to say no?
- Do you believe that being a boss to your child hurts her self-esteem?
- Do you believe families should be run like a democracy where parents and children are equals?
- Do you feel you spend too much time talking and explaining to your child and trying to persuade her to cooperate?
- Are you often embarrassed in public by your child's behavior?
- Do you dread mornings because your child hates to get up?
- Do you dread dinnertimes because your child always complains about whatever he is served?
- Do you worry that any mistake you make will result in permanent damage to your child?

The more times you answer yes, the more likely it is that you are caught in the trap of wimpy parenting.

Ask yourself this bottom-line question: Do you find yourself experiencing less and less pleasure as a parent while feeling increasingly burdened and frustrated?

CHAPTER 2

⸻〰〰⸻

The Wimpy Parent Epidemic

Every parent wants nice kids—kids who listen, behave, help out around the house, do their homework, and are fun to be with. Too many parents today feel frustrated in getting children to perform. Whenever I give talks, I often ask parents to raise their hands if:

- they really knock themselves out for their kids
- they are frustrated by how much their kids argue with them and are slow to cooperate.

As hands shoot up, there is a kind of anxious chuckle throughout the audience. Parents are no longer getting the results they expect: children show less respect, are more demanding, slower to cooperate, and harder to motivate.

Q: Why are so many of today's children so difficult to parent and teach?

A: The wimpy parent syndrome has propelled children into a position of authority.

The Child-Centered Parenting Movement

About twenty years ago, experts in the field of child development and psychology began to think there was a better way to raise children. Experts began to come up with "progressive" ideas that worked very well—on paper. Thanks to this movement the word "strict" became a dirty word in the world of parenting, and the very idea of punishment took on overtones of abuse.

The underlying notion was that *self-esteem was everything.* Parents were advised to promote good self-esteem in their children. Parents were encouraged to provide enrichment in the form of time and money, and the end result was guaranteed to be good self-esteem. The message was: The more services you perform, the better parent you are. You can't do enough good things for your kids.

The progressive idea was that *it is not good for children if parents act like their boss.* The assumption was that bossing children is ultimately a put-down and ends up harming their self-esteem. The antidote was a democratically run family with all members having equal votes. Parents were advised to talk things over, and reasoning with children became an obsession. Parents were encouraged to endlessly negotiate and to reach solutions through compromise. The end result was that parents who followed this course of action saw their own power totally diminished, and there were households full of argumentative children.

Parents were encouraged by the child-centered people to *teach their children to question authority* from an early age so they wouldn't grow up to be like robots who followed authority blindly. The result: a decline in respect for adult authority. Children, of course, do need to understand that all adults are not automatically right. However, we make a tremendous mistake if we raise children who have not learned to respect authority. As children mature and become more sophisticated, they can begin to learn that there are appropriate times when authority figures can be challenged.

The mission of child-centered parenting was to guide parents toward raising well-behaved children who would become successful, competent adults. This was the goal, but after over twenty years the living proof has been awful. "Awful" may not be a very scientific word, but awful behavior is what I observe and hear about as I interact with teachers, professionals in the field, parents, grandparents, police officers, and day-care center staffs. I recently witnessed an eight-year-old boy swear at his teacher on the grounds of a Catholic school. The teacher simply walked away in disgust. A substitute teacher told me she sent a ten-year-old boy to the principal's office for using strong curse words against her. The boy was returned to her class within twenty minutes with the explanation, "Oh, that's just how Bobby is." Grandparents cringe as they tell me stories of how their grandchildren run their parents. I'm now being asked to consult at day-care centers where children as young as two are described as out of control. Teachers close to retirement tell me how they can't wait to get out of the field because too many of today's children are no fun to be with. Psychologists all over the country spend a great deal of time these days correcting the consequences of so-called progressive child-centered parenting.

To summarize: What seemed like sophisticated and wise advice really ended up putting parents in a position that greatly diminished their authority. American parents were led to believe that being strict hurts the self-esteem of children and that children do better when parents stop being the boss and run the family as if it were a democracy. (This is particularly true of parents of only children who tend to treat their one child as an equal. It's hard to tell an equal to go to bed or brush his teeth.)

These ideas about being strict have not only been a failure, but they have made parenting an incredibly tough experience. When children do not respect their parents' authority, we see an assortment of behaviors that absolutely take the joy out of parenting. No one wins: parents and children both lose when parents fall into the wimpy parent trap.

What do children of wimpy parents look like?
- They are slow to cooperate.
- They make impudent and insulting comments to adults.
- They wheel and deal to get what they want.
- They never seem satisfied.
- They expect parents to be at their beck and call.
- They are poor at entertaining themselves.
- They think life is TV, McDonald's, and video games.
- They are rarely considerate of their parents' feelings.
- They rarely apologize.
- They have poor manners and social skills.
- They hate the word "no" and often have temper tantrums.
- They are very demanding.
- They are not much fun for a parent to be with!

Left-Behind Mom

One late fall afternoon, as I pulled into the parking lot of Toys "R" Us, I saw a ten-year-old boy jump out of his car and run into the toy store. I watched as his mom trudged through the parking lot after her son. A wimpy parent may not see the problem here. A parent who is in charge would know that what had happened was not quite right. The mother took time out to take her son to a toy store. The son didn't even have the courtesy to wait for his mom. Now the mom had to wander the aisles just to find him. I will guarantee you this boy did not thank his mom for taking him. This mom probably routincly feels that everything she does for her son is unappreciated.

Confessions of a Wimpy Parent

Trying not to be a wimpy parent is easier said than done. Parents who try to lay down the law inevitably back down in their new role as family cop, and then the kids really learn not to believe a word they say.

Here's a portion of a letter from a self-aware but wimpy parent:

> I have to figure out what makes me keep giving in and wimping out. I've read all the books by parenting experts, and a lot of what they suggest makes sense. After all, it's not brain surgery—it's parenting, and isn't that supposed to come naturally? What is going on inside of me that keeps me from changing my parenting style? If I find the key maybe I can shift gears and get back in the driver's seat and get control of my life and my kids' behavior.
>
> I want my kids to know how much I love and respect them. *I guess I believe that letting them call all the shots demonstrates respect. I also believe that if I come down too hard on them and don't let them get away with things, they will think I'm critical and demanding as opposed to loving.*

I want my kids to know that they are a top priority in my life. *I guess I believe that I always have to put them first and sacrifice my needs as a way of communicating their importance. I also think that if I do put myself first sometimes, I have to make up for it later. The old guilt trip!*

I have really good intentions and want to please my kids so they'll be happy. *Actually, kids have to learn how to deal appropriately with all kids of emotions, including anger, frustration, and disappointment. After all, as they begin to experience the realities of life, they will soon find out that everyone in the real world isn't going to be worried about making them happy.*

I want my kids to have fond memories of their childhood, not unpleasant ones where they remember how mad I always got at them. *Now that I think about it, I probably spend more time yelling and being aggravated at my kids than most of my friends who are not wimpy parents. When I give in all the time, things are really unpleasant for all of us.*

I'm afraid of the scenes my kids will create if I do try to lay down the law, especially in public or in front of guests. I don't know what is worse—having people think I'm a wimpy parent, or having them think my kids are brats. *I guess either way, my parenting skills aren't thought of very highly.*

The Epidemic

Several social events have made parents particularly vulnerable to wimpy parenting. The complexities of modern life conspire to leave many parents feeling guilty about their choices.

Should I put my children in a day-care center? What's our divorce doing to the kids? Should both parents work?

- **Divorced** parents often feel tremendous guilt over the divorce and how it hurts the children. They are reluctant to make their children's lives any more difficult or unhappy, so they easily give in to almost all requests and demands. Divorced fathers, in particular, don't want to spoil what little time they have with their children with discipline. As one dad said, "I only see my children four days a month and I don't want to take the chance of alienating them."
- **Fatigue** often helps nudge parents right into the wimpy parent trap. With both parents working full-time, often at very demanding careers, it is tempting to take the easy way out after a long day and cater to the children. Single-parent moms have a particularly difficult time finding the energy to be the sole provider and custodial parent; as a result single-parent mothers often fall behind with discipline.
- **Worry.** Parents are bombarded with information on the psychology of children. They worry they will make a critical mistake and end up damaging their kids for life. Parents wind up acting uncertain, hedging and backing down. Parents are almost immobilized by misleading articles that suggest that punishment causes children to feel unloved, worthless, or disconnected. This makes parents hesitate to respond and correct clearly inappropriate behavior.

Antidote

Wimpy parents can help lessen fatigue by not creating more work for themselves. When you stop giving in to your children's unreasonable demands, your workload will diminish significantly. (You won't be dashing to school with forgotten permission slips, or typing your child's latest research paper.)

Calm your guilt by knowing you will be making things much better for your children in the long run. When parents unwittingly put their children in charge, they often misbehave. The result is that parents feel even more guilt because now they feel like a failure. Wimpy parenting often creates a vicious cycle.

The irony is that although wimpy parents want a lot for their children, they are really handicapping them. The children of wimpy parents are overdemanding and argumentative, and their exaggerated sense of entitlement quickly dissolves into temper tantrums when they don't get their way.

CHAPTER 3

~vw~

How Not to Raise a Brat

Say the word "brat," and every parent instantly knows just the kind of kid you are talking about. Although no one intentionally sets out to raise a brat, we seem to have an abundance of bratty kids in our midst. The truth is that it is actually very easy to raise a brat.

I know, because even I fell into the brat trap.

Many years ago I was the father of a three-year-old daughter. Like most young parents, I used to feel very embarrassed when my daughter made a scene in public. It always felt like everyone was looking at me during those times and thinking, "Some psychologist he is. He can't even control his own kids." In public I unwittingly gave in to my daughter whenever she became bratty just to avoid a scene.

One afternoon my daughter and I entered a supermarket. We had just walked though the automatic doors when Connie spied a gigantic teddy bear way up on the shelf over the frozen food. If you didn't drive a station wagon, there wasn't a chance you could even get that thing home. But my little girl wanted that bear. At first I ignored her repeated requests. I tried to distract her to another part of the store. Finally I said, "No, we can't get the teddy bear." The word "no" seemed to be just too much, and she got this look in her eyes that said, "Boy are we going to have a scene now." Patiently I knelt down to talk with her in a rational way. (A clear indication of a wimpy response! Whoever heard of a three-year-old being rational?) At this point, Connie said something that was to change my parenting forever. She said, "If you don't get me that teddy bear, I'm going to scream and cry."

She was only three years old and she was manipulating me like a pro. She knew that I hated scenes in public, and she was taking advantage of this. Suddenly it hit me: I was creating a brat.

"No," I repeated, "you can't have that teddy bear. You can go ahead and scream, but we are still not getting it." She dissolved into a massive temper tantrum. Shoppers did stare, but this time I just didn't care. I took her out of the store. We both got into the car; my plan was to wait until she realized that her behavior was not going to work. The small space in the car just seemed to amplify her voice, and I found myself running out of patience. So I got out of the car and stood by the door. This was easier on my ears, and it also helped me to be more patient, since I wasn't suffering with all the yelling. Eventually Connie stopped crying when she discovered it wasn't working. I opened the door and said, "If you behave yourself now, we'll go finish our shopping."

I had learned an important lesson as a parent, and so had my daughter. She was on her way to understanding that miserable behavior was not going to pay off.

Love Is Blind

Have you ever noticed how the parents with the brattiest kids say nothing about their own little monsters, but fill your ears with tales about the brats down the street? As parents we think to ourselves, "Look who's talking!" That's because love is blind. When it comes to our own children, whom we love, we all have blind spots.

You certainly have heard another parent complain, "She's one of my best friends, but I just can't stand it when she brings those brats over." Or, "They are a terrific couple but never again will I have them in my house with those kids."

Picture this: Your close friend is visiting with you in your home, and you are trying to hold a conversation while one of her children is crawling up onto the bench of your newly upholstered piano with his dirty little Weeboks. Meanwhile the other youngster has wandered upstairs to explore the bedrooms. You watch as she disappears at the top of the stairs while your friend continues talking. Your attention is drawn from the top of the stairs to the piano by the wild chords being pounded out by her little brother.

Finally even your friend can't take the racket, so she attempts to restrain her son. He immediately collapses into a tempter tantrum, crying, shouting, and gagging simultaneously as he slams his little body on the floor. At this moment the explorer from upstairs reenters the scene. Her mouth is stuffed with candy she found in one of your children's rooms. Out of friendship, you try to ignore the scene and struggle to be pleasant. On the inside your nerves are being pulled so tight they are in danger of snapping. The little maestro has stopped the temper tantrum and is now clinging and whining to his mother with one demand after another. It's just impossible for you and your friend to go on talking with all the interruptions.

By now you are resenting your friend for bringing her two children into your home. Bratty kids definitely can put a strain on a friendship.

How (Not) to Make a Brat

The best way not to create a brat is to avoid the four most common mistakes. Once you learn the wrong (wimpy) way you will have greater confidence to do what is right.

Rarely point out the things your child is doing wrong.
The wimpy way: Be really permissive and let him get away with all sorts of questionable behavior. Try to be as patient and as accepting as possible. Say things like "Isn't he cute?" when he plays chemistry by mixing the orange juice with the chocolate milk. Or, throw up your hands: "What's a parent to do?"

The crucial point is that you don't want to give this little brat-in-training any idea he is bothering you or to stop and instruct him regarding what you do want him to do. A brat has never been taught that his behavior is troublesome for anyone or that it will lead to unpleasant consequences. A classic brat just enjoys himself at everyone else's expense. (Remember the trampoline brothers?)

Here's another brat story: One day I met with another psychologist over lunch to discuss professional matters. We had chosen a quiet restaurant frequented by businesspeople. We had just settled into our chairs when three young mothers entered the restaurant with their three preschoolers. The children immediately began to run around as if they were in a family-style restaurant like McDonald's. The mothers found a table and made themselves comfortable. By the time their wine had arrived, their children had managed to visit every table in the place. It didn't take a psychologist to see the growing annoyance among the customers and waitresses. These children were dishing out bratty behavior, totally oblivious to the effect they were having. But their parents never took the time to tell them.

After about half an hour, the mothers finally responded with a sharp "Get over here." Unfortunately, they didn't bother to point out the reason for the reprimand. These children never understood that they were having fun at the expense of at least twenty-five other people. To make matters worse, within minutes the kids were at it once again, and the parents were still ignoring them.

The better way: Let your child know when his behavior is upsetting to others. Give your child feedback with words, or use the time-out room. (See Section III for specific strategies.) Point out the reason for a reprimand. If a child is bothering everyone in a restaurant, it's not enough to just say, "Get over here." Explain, "There are people who came to have a quiet dinner and they can't do that if you continue to run around the tables."

When your child does something awful, respond by giving watered-down reprimands.

The wimpy way: "Just stop what you are doing" doesn't tell a child what is expected of her. If you sort of scold your child, but at the same time look at her adoringly, your words may express real disapproval, but your facial expression will be saying "You are really precious to me." In this manner your

scolding will be immediately washed away by your sweet, loving look. This convinces the child that you really don't mean
what you say. She won't believe for one moment that her
behavior is really a problem. Your attention and adoration will
encourage her to return to her bratty behavior before you can
blink your eyes.

Here's a scene that gets played out in my office at least
once a month: Right in the middle of one of my sessions with
a family, my office door swings open, and in races a three-year-
old or a four-year-old who has just escaped from his mother's
watchful eye. While Mother stands helpless in the doorway,
her little one makes a beeline for the toys in the far corner.
Mother is issuing a scolding in a singsong tone, half complaining and half amused. ("Oh, Doug, you little stinker,
come here. Dr. Condrell is going to be mad at you.") By now
little Doug has had access to the toys and is enjoying the game
of trying to avoid being caught by his mother, who is more
embarrassed than firm. Finally Doug is physically removed
from the office, but my session has been intruded on and
Doug has had one more lesson that bratty behavior pays off.
Doug has played with the toys and had the fun of Mother
chasing him.

The better way: Do not allow miserable behavior to pay
off. Stop the brat in her tracks. What lesson would my daughter Connie have learned that day if I had given her that teddy
bear? The lesson you want your child to learn is that good
things only happen when behavior is appropriate. And be
clear about the behavior you want to change. ("Doug, you
can't come into the doctor's office until you are invited in.")

Set limits and then quickly back off.

The wimpy way: You are usually wimpy in your scolding, but there comes a time when you can't stand it any longer, so you set a limit. Let's say your five-year-old is playing with the family car parked in the driveway at home. Sensing the potential danger of your car's being shifted into neutral and ending up on your neighbor's lawn, you remove the little fellow from the car and say no. You have just set a limit. You have taken action to stop some undesirable behavior. However, you immediately walk away or become involved in something else, so you don't see him sneak right back into the car. A good brat learns that if he persists, he can have his own way. The best way to teach him this lesson is to set a limit and naively go on to something else, never expecting your child to break your rule. Weak limit-setting teaches that persistence pays off.

The better way: Expect rules to be broken. Do not expect one-shot learning; children need many trials to learn the important lessons in life. For example, the first time you catch your little girl in the street with her tricycle you should expect that she will do it again, even if you scolded or punished her. The attraction of riding in the street is too tempting. Do not fool yourself into believing your teaching about not going into the street is over after one lesson. If you have a little girl and a bike, you need to periodically keep an eye on her, knowing that you will have to repeat the lesson when she goes into the street again.

Make sure you take your child everywhere you go.

The wimpy way: Say to yourself that childhood is just too precious, and you don't want to miss out on any of your little one's experiences. Where ever you go, he goes. Where ever he goes, you go. Never hire a baby-sitter. Continuously remind him just how important he is to you. You are teaching him that Mom and Daddy do not have a separate life apart from their children. A good brat is convinced he is at the center of everything and is more important than anyone else.

The better way: Make sure that your child knows that parenting is just one part of your life. A home that is too child-oriented gives a child an exaggerated sense of self-importance. Being a good parent doesn't mean you stop doing everything else.

All children, when they are very young, start off life being self-centered. For young children the theme is "Me, me, and more me." It's natural for children to see the world revolving around their needs and to feel that Mommy and Daddy are there just for their purposes. Young children know nothing about the demands of marriage, they have no idea that adults need time for their own hobbies and friends, and they never think that parents can take only so much time with kids.

However, little by little, with the help of parents, the self-centeredness can begin to be chipped away. Slowly a child learns that yes, she is important, but Mommy and Daddy have a special relationship apart from their relationship with her. At first, a child will have nothing to do with this idea. (Think back to the first time when you tried to leave the house with a baby-sitter in charge. Most parents have had to peel a child off their leg to get free and walk out the door.)

It's tough for kids to learn that parents have an adult life. It's also tough for parents not to go on promoting the children's fantasy that parents are there to always be close and to meet all of their needs.

This is just one more developmental task that children need their parents to teach them. Usually around the age of four or five, children finally catch on. If you are too caught up in your role as parent, your children will have a hard time succeeding with this lesson, and their sense of self-importance will remain unrealistically high.

CHAPTER 4

—◦◦◦—

The Secrets to Raising Successful Children

It is every parent's goal for her child to grow up to be a successful adult. Parents have considerable concern when they see their children acting in less than desirable ways. Conversely, parents feel reassured when they see their children doing their homework, completing household chores, or persevering through challenging tasks.

A sound family life provides children with the best classroom for learning how to run their own lives, which should be the goal of every parent. Developing a strong sense of personal responsibility in childhood is essential in helping children become prepared for the challenges of adult life in an often demanding and stressful world. Courage, responsibility, and cooperation—the three qualities at the heart of a healthy personality—are all intertwined and are best learned in the family. When we look at people who have it all together and who are successful, we see them demonstrate these three qualities over and over again.

Courage

When I talk about courage I'm not talking about the kind of courage that sustains a fireman who rescues a baby from a burning home. I'm talking about the courage it takes to hang in there when the going gets tough. The child who learns to get up and try again after life has knocked him down has learned a very powerful lesson. Courage means not quitting when life gives you a kick. It means not being afraid to try new things. Often successful people aren't always the smartest, but they are those who persist and hang in there. Because our world is a competitive one filled with frustrations, quitters have a terrible time in our society.

To develop courage, promote self-confidence.

- Encourage your child to take risks and try activities he is not sure of. Succeeding at new things gives self-confidence a real boost.
- Teach your child skills she never practiced before. The more your child knows, the more confident she becomes.
- Be supportive. When the going gets tough say, "You're on your way." Or, "Good try."
- Enjoy your child. Confidence grows when a child knows he is important to his mom and dad.
- Reward your child when she doesn't quit the moment she is discouraged.
- Ask your child's opinion. Kids often have great ideas, and when adults ask for them, their confidence is enhanced.

Responsibility

When they hear the word "responsibility," parents think about children making their beds and taking out the garbage. I'm thinking about a youngster's ability to admit and face up to his own mistakes. It is so easy and painless to blame others. Children have to move beyond that if they are going to grow.

Communicate to your child that mistakes are opportunities for learning, changing, for improving and growing. They are not events to be ashamed of or covered up. The losers in life are the blamers: Everyone else is always responsible for the way their life is. The mature person can see mistakes and profit from them. A child who is responsible can accept the consequences of her behavior and learn how to act differently next time. The children of wimpy parents rarely say "I was wrong" or "I goofed."

Do make your child live up to her commitments.

Last week Lois was waiting for her neighbor's daughter Jane to baby-sit. Lois opened the door, and there was Jane's mother. "Where's Jane?" asked Lois. The mother responded, "Oh, she had a date she didn't want to miss. So I'll baby-sit for you."

Let your kids practice responsibility. Parents shouldn't expect their children to learn responsibility without giving them plenty of opportunity to practice acting in a responsible manner. Involve your children in age-appropriate household chores. Even children as young as two and three years of age can participate to some extent in chores. Toddlers can be asked to bring their cup to the sink after a meal or to pick up their stuffed animals from the floor and put them up on their bed. Certainly older children can help set the table prior to meals, help clear the table, take out garbage, and so on.

Parents can borrow from the experience of teachers, who know how important it is to break tasks down into small incremental steps, to provide periodic feedback during performance, to model or offer to demonstrate, and to help children identify options in the face of challenges.

The important part is that the child begins to learn the lessons of responsibility at an early age. A life of leisure without any focus on duty or work will not help a child develop a sense of responsibility. This is a learning process. Positive reinforcement, especially in the form of genuinely expressed praise in response to the child's display of responsible behavior, is extremely important.

Cooperation

Cooperation means getting along with other people. Life takes on special meaning as we grow in our capacity to enjoy people and relate to them in a give-and-take way. Learning how to make friends and to keep them is what cooperation is all about.

Do provide feedback to your child. "I was watching what you did when you were disappointed earlier—that was a pretty good response." If there are problems, ask, "What will you do when that happens again?"

Encourage friendships. Successful people have friends. Yet this is an area often overlooked by parents, because play is something considered to be nice but not necessary. But keep in mind that children are not born with the social skills they need to make and keep friends.

Children need to be taught how to get along with others.

- Expose your child to other children from an early age.
- Gently and supportively correct your child's social behavior when it's out of line. If he is cheating, calling names, or acting like a bully, he needs to hear from you in a manner that isn't so harsh he blocks you out.
- Encourage skills that help make your child an attractive playmate. The more things a child can do, the more interesting she becomes as a companion. Boring children have very few skills for having fun.
- Set a good example at home in the way both parents treat each other. Model consideration, thoughtfulness, giving, patience, and sharing.
- Be open to having children come to your home to play. Encourage your child to reach out to other children.

Feedback: Teaching Sensitivity

Children periodically need to get information on how their behavior is coming across and affecting others. When a child looks into a mirror, she gets feedback on how she looks. When a child behaves correctly or misbehaves, she has no mirror to look into unless her parents take time to give her feedback. When parents reflect back to a child how she is coming across, they are acting as a mirror for that child.

This takes time. All children, no matter what their ages, need feedback on their behavior.

Sometimes the feedback comes as praise. "I like the way you shared with your friend," says a parent. Sometimes the feedback is a scolding: "I'm very upset and angry that you took my money off the dresser without asking. That is wrong," admonishes a father. Sometimes the feedback consists of trying to get your youngster to feel for the other person. "How do you think your friend felt when you called him a name and screamed at him to go home?" asks a mother. At other times the feedback is ignoring behavior as long as it isn't hurting anyone or resulting in any physical damage. "Until you stop whining, I am not going to talk with you or give you any attention," explains a mother. And of course sometimes the feedback is punishment. "Because you lied to me about finishing your homework, you are going to bed one hour earlier this week as a punishment," says a father.

There are several ways to give your child feedback on his behavior. When my son was eight years old, one of his friends came over to play with him. I remember it as a cold, rainy day because I was so impressed at the time that this little boy walked about three blocks just to play with my son. "Can you play?" the rain-soaked boy asked my son. "No," said my son, who proceeded to close the door in the boy's face. "What are you doing?" I asked. "You don't treat a friend that way." My son looked completely confused at my reaction. I explained to him, "It's special when someone reaches out to you by walking over to your house and asking you to play. It means he likes you enough to walk over in the rain. You don't just close the door in someone's face when he shows that kind of interest in you."

I went on to point out various ways my son could have acted: "You could have asked him into the house to talk with him a little. You could have explained that you don't want to play today, but maybe tomorrow. You could have thanked him for coming over." My son listened, but he looked annoyed, as if to say, "So what's the big deal? He came over and I didn't want to play." But at least I know he heard me. I was satisfied at the time, because I understood that children don't catch on with just one lesson. I expected, correctly, that I would have to give my son feedback again on how to treat a friend, until his sensitivity to others was better developed. Children rarely learn good social skills with just one trial.

Giving a child feedback is also one of the best ways to help a youngster tune in on how he may be defeating himself. Gentle feedback helps a child deal with self-defeating behavior when you provide information to the child in a supportive way: "You know, Bobby, lately you have been doing a lot of complaining. Let's see if you can do less of that." A youngster might need feedback on other behaviors such as bragging, crying, whining, or calling names.

The ABCs of Success: Natural Consequences

Wimpy parents often don't let their children experience any of life's hard knocks or frustrations. They cheerfully let them off the hook. ("I know you are tired, so you don't have to practice the piano today." "If you don't want to try out again for the squad, that's OK—they shouldn't have turned you down.")

Fourteen-year-old Annie ignored an overflowing toilet overnight, so that in the morning the new carpet in her bedroom was soaked. Her parents arranged to have the carpet picked up and sent out to be cleaned. In order for that to be done, stacks of books in the room had to be moved and stored in boxes. So her parents hired neighborhood kids to do the job, while Annie just relaxed. Her mom was quick to explain: "It wasn't her fault; she didn't mean to ruin the carpet." It was an accident, but that doesn't mean Annie couldn't acknowledge her role and pitch in.

As loving parents, we are misguided when we keep our children from learning about life through dealing with natural consequences—those things that happen to you as a result of your own behavior. ("If you stay up too late, chances are you will feel tired tomorrow.") Natural consequences can teach us that we have to make some changes in our lives. When we eliminate them from our children's lives we are cheating them, although we justify our behavior by saying we do this because we love them. We should be helping our children tune in to the harsher melody of life.

In terms of your daily parenting behavior it means you look for natural consequences or opportunities to help your children learn. If your child has forgotten his lunch for the fifth time and calls you from school, don't rush over. One or two afternoons of going hungry might help him think ahead. Let's say your child persists in not getting out of bed, and each morning is a tug-of-war. Let him be late. Call the principal or teacher and let them know that you will be bringing your child in when he is ready. The child will have to face the principal and his teacher. You might even make him go to bed earlier. If you are thinking "But I can't be mean to my children," you are on the way to falling into the wimpy parent trap and staying stuck. Better you should be mean to your children now before life is mean to them and the consequences are big and painful. ("I have to let you go, because you consistently show up late for work.")

A: Children need to make personal choices. Children are confronted with numerous situations in which choices or decisions need to be made in the absence of parents or other adult authority figures. Allow your child the opportunity to make safe age-appropriate choices. Anticipate situations in which the child has the opportunity to make a choice or decision.

The really hard part is experiencing the consequences of one's choices. This is the critical element in the process of responsibility development. Parental guilt often underlies a parent's tendency to shield his child from consequences: he feels that his child acted irresponsibly due to something he as a parent did or did not do. Children are quick to pick up on this and use it to hold the parent accountable for their actions. ("Dad, if you had gone to the library for me like I asked, the report would have been better.")

B: Teach coping skills. When a child is frustrated but does not have a temper tantrum, she is coping. When a child is hungry and dinner is an hour away, she's coping if she waits patiently or goes off to play. If a child is being teased by a group and she quietly withdraws, that child is coping. It means managing your feelings and staying in control. It means working things out.

When you see your child coping, make sure to praise him. Say things like "Hey, you handled that OK." "Nice going." "I'm proud of the way you worked that out." Statements like these encourage a child to go on finding ways to handle the ups and downs in life.

Ask your child questions after you see that she has tried to cope and it hasn't come out too well. "What might you do the next time that happens?" "You know that will probably happen again—what will you do then?" Or, "Was there any other way you could have handled that?" Invite your child to participate in thinking up ways of handling something. Always provide feedback for your child, but don't be over-protective.

C: Children must learn to control their feelings. Children must learn that they are responsible for their thoughts and feelings and that properly channeled thoughts and feelings can help them make responsible and healthy choices. Children feel that other people "make" them feel or behave in a certain way. For example, children often say, "It's *your* fault I'm mad. I wouldn't be mad if you didn't make me clean my room." Parental limits or directives can understandably precipitate anger in a child, but the child needs to realize that it is a matter of personal choice whether to accept the rule and act cooperatively or respond with anger and defiance. Children need to be taught that no one can make them feel or behave in a particular manner. They choose how they will react.

The Ungrateful Child

A successful child is an appreciative one. One of the ideas that gets parents into trouble is that good parents should knock themselves out for their kids. Some progressive parenting gurus encourage parents to think that the more they do for their children, the better they are as parents. This has resulted in a lot of parents who are running their kids all over the place to enrich their lives and are ending up with kids who are selfish, demanding, and ungrateful. This approach results in kids who are never satisfied.

Scenario: You are a good dad who wants to bond with his son. You are going to take him to watch his favorite hockey team. You even sweeten the deal by letting him invite a friend along, and you take them both to have dinner on the way to the game at their favorite fast food hangout. Once at the game, you spring for a program and popcorn and soda pop. You are bonding with your son, and the boys are having a ball. On the way home your son asks you to stop so he and his friend can have ice cream. You say no because it's getting late and they have had enough to eat. At this moment your son explodes: "You never let me do what I want." The kid starts to turn mean. Not only has he not thanked you for the evening, but now he is complaining because you dared to turn down one of his requests. Welcome to the nineties and to kids who are never satisfied.

This is how I would recommend the father handle his son:

Let your son know that his behavior is unacceptable. Pick a time when your son has quieted down. Then say something like "I love you; you're a neat kid, but what you did last night was unacceptable. I was very disappointed in your behavior."

Explain the facts of life to your son. Parents have to provide their children with the basics—food, clothing, and shelter. Everything else a parent does is called an "extra." Extras include going to the hockey game, getting roller skates, attending a movie, taking karate lessons, and so on. In most homes, the list of extras is endless. The father in this example needs to explain to his son that when parents do extras for him he should show his appreciation by saying "thank you" and should not pile on more demands.

Set limits on your child's ungrateful behavior. After enduring ungratefulness, set a limit. "Son, there will be no extras for the next two weeks." The purpose of setting limits is both to punish your child and to help him experience how much he misses when you stop shelling out the extras. After two weeks, the extras can come back, with the warning that they will continue only as long as he shows appreciation with words and with actions, in the form of helping out around the house. The lesson here is that life is a two-way street: "We do for you and you do for us." The wimpy parent says, "We do for you and we do for you, and you don't have to do anything in return because you are just a kid."

CHAPTER 5

—∾—

Raising Moral Children in Today's World

Some experts fear we are in danger of raising a generation of moral illiterates. A recent national survey revealed that 33 percent of high school students had shoplifted in the past twelve months, and a whopping 61 percent admitted to having cheated on an exam. Many children today behave as if they have no internal moral guidance system.

It's up to parents to provide the compass for our children to follow. We need to teach children such values as honesty, self-control, and respect for authority.

When Marcia picked up her ten-year-old son, Seth, from school one Friday, she could instantly see that he was upset. He handed her a letter that congratulated him for winning the fifth-grade reading contest and invited him and his family to a reception the following Tuesday. All year the students had been engaged in a read-a-thon sponsored by the school librarian, tracking weekly the number of pages they had read. When

Marcia asked Seth why he was upset that he won, he said, "Mom, I didn't deserve to win; I cheated." It turned out that when the librarian had collected the read-a-thon sheets on Wednesday, Seth just filled in the rest of the read-a-thon page as if he had finished the last book. He had no idea that it was actually a contest. (In fact, none of the letters to parents about the read-a-thon had ever described it as a contest.)

Seth's mom knew this was an important moment, and she didn't want to blow it. Together she and Seth carefully listed Seth's options: Seth could do and say nothing and just show up on Tuesday. He could spend the weekend reading all the pages he had pledged to read, and then he would deserve the honor. Or he could turn down the award.

Seth decided to write a letter to the school librarian, explaining that he hadn't read the last fifty pages in the last book. On Monday his mom made sure the letter got into the librarian's mailbox. Mom told Seth that she was really proud of him and supported his decision to come clean, but she warned him that the librarian might be very upset and might even want to punish him. Seth came home from school beaming. The librarian was very impressed with his honesty, and she told him that he would have won the read-a-thon anyway, even without those last fifty pages. She even kissed him (!) which he pronounced "yucky." Mom, Dad, and Seth all enjoyed the reception on Tuesday.

Seven Ways to Raise a Moral Child

1. Tell your children what you value. Children need to hear from their parents about the importance of honesty and self-discipline and being responsible. Be sure to praise your children when they choose the right path. ("I am so proud that you returned the extra money the storekeeper gave you by mistake.")

2. Have your children think about how the other person feels. Teach empathy, the recognition of another person's feelings. A child with empathy, who recognizes the impact of her behavior on others, is more likely to treat others well. When parents teach their children to think about how the other person feels, they have taken a giant step toward raising moral children.

Teach your child to ask herself these two questions:

"How do you think your friend felt when you . . . ?" and "How do you think you should behave the next time when this happens?"

3. Build trust and optimism. A positive attitude about life will steer a child in one direction, while a negative attitude will steer a child somewhere else. The child who believes that people are more likely to be kind than mean to him will be more open to other people. The child who sees his glass of chocolate milk as half full rather than half empty will have the advantage of seeing the world for what it offers rather than what it takes away. As a parent, make sure you are not a complainer who always expects the worst.

Keep promises. In general, if you make a promise, make every effort to follow through. Be truthful and avoid deception. Encourage your children to participate and become involved in the joys of life.

4. Let your children know it is OK to occasionally do something wrong. It's important to acknowledge the misstep. If the consequences are too severe, children will lie whenever they misbehave and will almost never admit to being at fault. (See chapter 15.) Recognize the power of guilt.

Unfortunately many parents have generalized that all guilty feelings are bad. In fact, guilt can be helpful. (It was the nagging voice of Seth's conscience that told him he didn't deserve that award.) Guilty feelings are signals that we did or are about to do something wrong.

You may need to help your children feel guilty over some aspect of their behavior. Teach your child that the best way to get rid of the guilt is to make things up to the person she just wronged: "Do you know the trouble you caused your friend by lying? He is getting punished by his parents for something you did. You need to fix it."

A mother was walking two seven-year-olds home from school and stopped into a candy store to buy them juice. When she got outside she saw that both boys had candy in their hands. They admitted they had taken some loose candy, but said, "It was just a little candy. They won't miss it." The mom insisted the boys go back and offer to pay for the candy.

5. Take a stand. There will be many times when you will have to make decisions not popular with your kids. Maybe you don't want your child to go to a certain movie; you need a response to the proverbial "But all my friends are going to see it. . . ." If you know your fourteen-year-old will be going to a party where beer is served, you have the obligation to say no and not to be wimpy.

6. Tell your children stories about heroes. Stories about heroes can inspire children to behave in ways that are strong and admirable. I still recall that when I was a child my teachers read stories about real heroes that made my friends and me want to grow up to be just like them. Understand that your children's definition of "hero" is usually synonymous with someone who has achieved fame and fortune. (Madonna and Michael Jordan are mentioned frequently as "heroes" by teens.) Find other kinds of heroes to teach your children about.

7. Let your life be your message. Parents can give their children powerful messages about behavior simply by being positive role models. Children learn a lot by watching their parents interact with each other. Show affection by touching as well as with words. Let your children see your disagreements, but make sure they also see how you resolve your differences and make up. Be thoughtful and sensitive to each other's needs and express your feelings. Share and give to each other and, above all, communicate. Your children will watch you like two actors on a stage. Give them a good "performance," and they can't help but develop into the best kind of adults.

Being a Role Model

Young children are the greatest copycats in the world—that is how a lot of socialization happens. That is why every preschool has a corner stocked with grown-up clothes so kids can dress like Mom and Dad and play house and school and pretend to be like big people.

A mother recently consulted with me about her eight-year-old daughter who, she felt, didn't respect her. Although the mother thought she was making a good effort to teach her daughter values, she found her little girl to be disrespectful and disobedient. During one of my session with the little girl, she said, "Can I ask you some questions?" "Sure," I said. "How come my mother lies?" she asked. "I saw her with her boyfriend the other day and she said that wasn't her, but I know that was my mom." Then she asked,

"How come she swears and hits the wall with her fist?" I began to understand, only too well, why the mom—who seemed like a nice enough woman—was having such a hard time building respect. The mom was figuratively shooting herself in the foot. Although Mom wanted to be respected, her daughter was seeing a mom who lied, swore, and put dents in the wall.

Parents can have a tremendous impact on their children just by being the kind of person they are. The problem with some wimpy parents is that they have lowered their standards for what is correct behavior, and the children copy the lowered standards. The same parents who have lowered their standards of what is correct act shocked when they see their children behave in thoughtless and uncaring ways.

Recently I was asked to introduce Sesame Street characters to an audience of over 2,600 parents and kids for a show called *Let's Play School*. The show took place in one of Buffalo's old movie houses with a history that goes all the way back to vaudeville. My job was to introduce the 4:30 P.M. performance. I arrived at the theater just as the audience was leaving from the 2:30 performance. This theater holds so many memories for me that I couldn't resist walking in to look at this breathtaking old movie house before the audience for the next performance arrived. The door closed behind me, and I looked out over the thousands of empty seats. My special moment of excitement was lost in a feeling of despair. My eyes were glued to the tons of garbage left in the theater. Ushers were busy scurrying to sweep each row of debris. In the aisles were huge garbage bags filled with mountains of popcorn boxes, cups, wrappers, napkins, and other clutter.

Just moments before, I had watched hundreds of parents

leave this place with their young children. I was touched by the love I felt and I was impressed at parents' going out of their way on Sunday to show their children a great time. But now I was looking at this theater littered with debris and asking myself: "What is wrong with this picture?" What was so wrong was that these loving parents were exposing their children to bad behavior. The adult message they were sending was:

- We don't have to respect the property of others.
- It doesn't matter if we go into a special place and mess it up with our garbage.
- It doesn't matter if our behavior inconveniences others and makes more work for them.
- Being neat and picking up after ourselves is not all that important.

I'm sure that most of the parents who were there that day were oblivious to how they had communicated all these poor lessons to their children.

Responsible parents need to hold their children to certain standards of good behavior.

"No, you can't drop your gum wrapper on the floor and walk away." "From now on, you knock before you come into our room." "We don't eat with our fingers. Here is a fork." "You need to tell Grandma you're sorry for what you said to her."

Building Respect Through Teaching Manners

When I interview teachers about their views on today's children and respect, I almost always get this answer: "It's nonexistent."

The secret to building respect in children is to teach them manners. Some parents will think, "What does using a napkin or choosing the right fork have to do with respect?" Manners involve a lot more than choosing the right fork or using a napkin rather than a shirtsleeve. When we teach children manners, we teach children to be considerate of others, to think of other people's feelings, and to treat others thoughtfully. When you teach them all of this you are also teaching them the way you expect them to treat you.

- How do you feel when you see someone toss a piece of garbage out of their car window?
- How do you feel when you step on someone's gum and you have to stand on one leg trying to scrape the stuff off your shoe?
- How do you feel when you sit down in the movie theater and you feel the crunch of someone's popcorn underneath your feet and see the floor cluttered with napkins, cups, and wrappers?
- How do you feel when you are stuck in traffic and you read a bumper sticker on the car in front of you that reads "If you don't like my driving, call 1 800 GO TO HELL"?
- How do you feel when you are carrying an armload of bags and you can't open the door to leave the mall and four people standing right in front of you do not offer to help?

The answer is: It doesn't feel very good at all. People like to be treated with respect. When you teach your children to be respectful you are giving them a head start in life, and you are also making your life as a parent easier and more rewarding.

This past winter I was vacationing on one of the islands in the Bahamas. One morning, while I was stretched out on a lounge enjoying the sun, sand, and sea, I heard a youngster ask, "Can I help you?" I looked up to see an eleven-year-old boy volunteering to help a woman who was struggling to carry her lounge chair closer to the beach. I was impressed because that kind of behavior is rare today. When the boy's parents arrived I complimented them on their son's thoughtfulness and good manners. The father said, "We stress manners in our house. In fact, last week I sent two of my son's friends home because they were swearing and being rude."

This story highlights some important points:

- We are attracted to people with good manners.
- People with good manners impress us as being respectful.
- People with good manners are appreciated.
- Parents teach good manners at home by setting standards of good behavior.
- Children who have good manners are naturally respectful.

Over the years I have seen many children who were unhappy because they had a difficult time making and keeping friends. The one thing all these children had in common was a total lack of manners. So I started their treatment by teaching them how to say "please" and "thank you" and how to ask for permission and how not to grab for the cookies during snack time and not to burp and to knock before opening a

door and to shake hands and be helpful to others and to apologize—the list is endless. I have earned a reputation as a child
psychologist who helps children who were loners to become
popular. I couldn't have succeeded without the lessons on
manners.

SECTION II

Taking Charge

INTRODUCTION

In order to be an effective parent you need to be a kind, loving, benevolent dictator. If "dictator" is too strong a word for you, then try "boss." You need to be your children's boss.

The words "discipline" and "strict" have become equated with meanness. But this connection is not correct. "Discipline" means "teaching" and "strict" means that you follow through with what you say you are going to do if a rule is broken.

I suggest that parents take a pledge to help stay focused on what their job is as a parent.

The Parent Pledge

- I am a loving parent.
- It is up to me to prepare my children for life.
- I am my children's teacher and coach.

- Home is my children's classroom for learning the basic lessons of life.
- My children's mistakes are my opportunities to teach them a better way.
- The lessons I teach my children can only be taught if I am their leader and they respect me.

CHAPTER 6

—◦◦◦—

How to Be an Effective Parent

Self-Esteem

As we've seen, parents in the 1990s have come to believe that building self-esteem is crucial. They have been told they must do everything possible to "give" their children self-esteem. Parents today believe that they can hurt their children's self-esteem by bossing them, by upsetting them with reprimands, by making them feel guilty when they have done something wrong, or by punishing them at all. Some experts have actually warned that punishment can make children grow up feeling rootless and disconnected. This misguided statement has to strike terror in the hearts of parents. No parent wants to raise a rootless child! All this advice does is to erode the authority of parents.

First of all, understand that you can't *give* children self-esteem. Today it is not uncommon to see children coming home from preschool with a sticker on their shirt declaring

"I'm number one." Some educators seem to believe that if you constantly tell kids they are number one you are building self-esteem. Unfortunately this daily mantra is disconnected from any act of competence. Self-esteem doesn't come from saying "You're wonderful" or "You're number one." After a while a child becomes indifferent to all these nice statements.

Children only gain self-esteem by experiencing their own competence. As children learn how to make and keep friends, their self-esteem grows; they feel like valued and desired people. As children earn good grades, do chores, and help out their families they build self-esteem. As they accumulate figurative "stars" as a result of their own actions, their self-esteem will shine.

You are not going to damage your children's self-esteem by providing them with discipline. It is your job to make your children unhappy by denying them an ice-cream cone just before dinner. It is your job to let them feel guilty when they take their friends' crayons and they insist they did nothing wrong. It is even your job to punish them when all else has failed. You are not on the path to ruining your child's self-esteem.

It's even OK if your kids are a little afraid of you. Of course a child should not fear that his parents are going to physically hurt him. A child should never cower and raise his hands in self-defense as if his parents are going to strike him when they scold. A child should not fear being abandoned or rejected. But it is OK for a child to be afraid that if he misbehaves he will end up disappointing his parents and he will be punished. The parent is a powerful person in the life of a child. The child wants to impress his parents and win their praise. It is not a toxic or traumatic thing for a child to be fearful about breaking parents' rules. Fear has a place in helping people to behave properly. Look at the adult world for a moment. Many employees fear their boss may fire them if they don't follow the rules at work. We drive our cars with some fear that we will get a ticket if we speed.

The Right Attitude

Without discipline, you will experience a lot of bratty behavior that will not make you proud of your children and will even make you feel like a failure as a parent. Parents who have bought into the wimpy parent syndrome often come up with excuses for avoiding discipline:

- I hate to upset my children.
- It is so hard for me to say no.
- I'm afraid they won't love me.
- I worry I'll damage them.
- I feel guilty because I have to work.
- I don't want to spoil what little time we have.
- I feel sorry for them.

When any of these excuses pop into your head, repeat the following: "If I don't discipline my children, the world will. And the world will not be so loving."

If you don't direct your children they will not be ready for the world outside their home. They will then have to learn the lessons of life the hard way from people who don't love them as you do. Lessons such as:

- Being on time
- Keeping promises

- Respecting authority
- Telling the truth
- Cooperating with others
- Sharing and helping out
- Working hard
- Postponing gratification
- Taking pride in accomplishments
- Learning from mistakes
- Following the rules
- Obeying laws
- Knowing right from wrong
- Apologizing and making up for mistakes

Love Is Not Enough

I have been counseling Billy, the only son of two very nice but wimpy parents. When Billy was a youngster, he had no set bedtime. He went to sleep when he felt like it and wherever he wanted to, which was often in front of the TV in the family room. He rarely chose to eat at the dinner table with his two sisters, and if he didn't like what his mom had prepared she would simply make him an alternate meal. When Billy's parents occasionally tried to stick to a rule, he would carry on a campaign of harassment so they would back down. He manipulated his parents and he did the same with his teachers. In fact, Billy hated school because his teachers were always trying to tell him what to do.

By the time Billy came to me he was a depressed, angry, and belligerent teenager. He was miserable because he had no preparation for the real world. He hated his parents, who now had decided to become stricter. For the first time Billy's parents were asking him to help out around the house (his sisters were tired of "Prince Billy" getting out of chores), to do his homework, and to get to bed at a reasonable time. Billy was outraged by these demands, of course. He responded with indignation. He often gave his parents the finger and used the F word. Billy's parents had raised a misfit. He couldn't even keep a job at the supermarket because he showed up late. His friends were other immature teens, since kids who had their act together were not attracted to Billy.

Billy's parents had mistakenly thought that if they gave him love and indulgence, they would be rewarded with a son who was respectful, cooperative, and loving and who liked himself. Time after time, I find that the most unhappy children are the children who grew up calling all the shots. Love is not enough for parenting a child.

Update: Billy did improve over time. For a while after high school, he lost one job after another because he was unreliable and antagonistic to his bosses. Finally through a combination of the school of hard knocks and counseling, Billy started college at twenty-two. He entered the field of hotel management and now at twenty-seven is experiencing real success both personally and professionally.

Golden Rule: Discipline and love go together.

Discipline begins with a good parent-child relationship. I can teach you a lot of discipline strategies to help your children learn how to behave, but if your children do not love you, all the discipline strategies in the world won't work. The chemistry of love has to be there to connect child and parent together.

The next time you play with your child, or hug and kiss him, or tell him how much you love him, or comfort him when he is upset, make sure to say to yourself, "All of this nurturing and love is part of discipline." Children who feel loved and cared for have a desire to please their parents and to impress them with their achievements.

As we've seen, love is not enough to raise good children. Some parents believe all you have to do is love them and they will do whatever you want and will magically grow up to be responsible, caring, mature, successful adults. But the love a parent feels and shows a child must also be accompanied by efforts to teach the child the lessons of life. The two Ls of good parenting are Love and Leadership.

A few years ago I spent a day touring a boot camp facility in Florida. This boot camp was somewhere between a prison and a school and was designed to help teenagers who were living a life of crime. These kids were all three-time convicted felons. I talked with many of these kids, who had been convicted of crimes like arson and drive-by shootings. I said to each one, "Tell me about your family." Kid after kid responded, "I have no family." Some gave details ("My dad is in prison, and I don't know where my mother went.") These kids were missing both love and leadership.

The Two Most Common Mistakes Parents Make

1. **Parents do not parent their children as a team.** In two-parent homes there should be two authority figures. When

Mom and Dad are on the same team, parenting becomes a lot easier because children listen better when they get the same message from the two most important people in their lives. If, however, one parent says one thing while the other parent says another, the children will either ignore you both or side with the parent who offers the best deal.

One of the biggest problems is the "Mommy knows best" syndrome. All too often I see mothers concluding that there is only one way to give a kid juice, and one way to put on a diaper, bathe a child, and so on. The one way is Mom's way. Women, it's said, have the instinct for mothering. This makes Mom very critical of Dad's efforts to care for the children. It doesn't take the average man very long to say, "OK, if you know best, then *you* do it." Dad essentially retires from much of the caregiving, and Mother is now on overload.

The solution is that each parent has to become aware that there may be different approaches to handling the kids. The important thing for parents to understand is that two parents actively involved in the caregiving activities of parenting make for happier kids and a stronger marriage.

I was counseling a mother about all the arguing between her and her husband concerning child care. Since this mom was very much into the "Mommy knows best" syndrome, I encouraged her to let her husband be alone with the children. I gave her the assignment of going shopping one night and letting Dad put the kids to bed. A week went by, and this mom returned to my office very upset. She couldn't wait to tell me how her husband had "failed." "Do you know what he did?" she snapped. "He put the children to bed in their summer pajamas in the middle of winter." I said, "Tell me, how did the kids make out that night with their dad?" She answered, "Oh, they had a wonderful time, and they are still talking about the pillow fight and all the fun they had." "So what's the problem?" I asked. I could practically see the light turn on over her head. When I asked her what she was thinking, she responded, "Men and women have different ways of doing things with kids, so why not accept this rather than constantly fighting over it?"

Compounding "Mommy knows best" is that Dad hates having the role of Mom's helper, and Mom hates having all the responsibility for running the home. Each parent has gripes. The situation of Dad's being Mom's helper creates a lot of resentment between parents. In turn, it fuels disagreements on how the kids should be parented. To solve this problem, Dad has to become more aware of how much more work his wife does with the children.

To do this, parents may use Dr. Ron Toffel's method, described in his book *Why Parents Disagree*. Each parent keeps a diary for a couple of days of all interactions with the children. At the end of two or three days, Mom and Dad should meet to share their lists. I guarantee that Mom will have written a small book and Dad will have a page or two. The light should go on for Dad at this moment. And Mom should begin to think, "My husband needs to be my partner and not have the demeaning role of my helper in this family." Both parents can begin to realign their relationship. Mom needs to be willing to let go of some of her responsibilities, and Dad needs to be willing to pick up some of the slack. When he is doing more, Dad needs to say to himself, "I'm not helping out, I'm doing this for myself because it brings me closer to the children and makes for a happier home."

2. **Parents spend too much time being parents** and not enough time being a couple. I often advise parents, "Do your children a favor and get away from them." A big problem I

see in my practice is that many mothers and fathers have no life of their own. Some rationalize this by saying, "Childhood is so precious, I don't want to miss a single second with the children." I have a hard time not gagging when I hear this one. The honest parent will recognize that no matter how much you love your children, you can't stand them sometimes, and you need a break from parenting.

Some parents justify never having a vacation or never going out because they can't find anyone they would trust with their kids. I assure you: You can find trustworthy sitters. You interview sitters; you call up references and then you have the candidates sit with your children while you are in the house so you can see them in action. This may sound like a lot of work—and it is—but compared to getting a divorce and starting all over, it is a piece of cake.

The most important relationship in the family is the relationship between Mom and Dad. As the marriage goes, so does the family. Also be aware that the couple having significant marital problems will fight each other through the children. If you recognize this as your situation, get some professional counseling. (See chapter 9 for more advice.)

CHAPTER 7

—◦◦◦—

How to Set Limits

I am counseling a mother with a nine-year-old boy who has a behavior problem both in school and at home. One of the behaviors that bothers her the most is that he never returns home on time. Each night he casually wanders in late for dinner. After a brief scolding, Mom makes sure he has what he wants to eat. Of course he doesn't like what Mom prepares so she makes him his favorite, a grilled cheese sandwich. I ask this mom to tell me how she thinks she could correct this situation. She replies, "I'll buy him a watch, so he can tell what time it is." It is hard for this mom to understand that what this kid needs is for his parents to set limits. He needs a rule and a consequence. ("You cannot be more than ten minutes late for dinner. If you are, the punishment will be that you will get no dinner, and you will go to bed early.")

One of the most important things that a parent can do is to set firm, age-appropriate limits on her child's behavior. Children need external limits, especially in early childhood, since young children do not have the ability to regulate their own emotions, behaviors, and desires.

Children cannot learn self-control without initially experiencing consistent control exerted by an external authority figure. Limit setting by parents helps children develop a capacity for self-discipline that becomes the foundation of responsibility development in later years.

Limit setting is good for parents—it prevents mental and physical exhaustion—but it is also good for the personality development of the child. All children need borders to the world they live in and parents who help set the borders for them. Children without limits often feel anxious and fear they will be out of control.

Let me introduce you to Michael, the only child of doting parents. When he was younger, his parents carried him everywhere. He had all of the most expensive toys, which he often threw at his parents. Michael is now a fourteen-year-old who has trouble getting up in the morning, which is common at his age. What is not common is that in order to accommodate him, his father brings him breakfast in bed and helps him dress. Michael's parents have even arranged to have a car service waiting because he doesn't get up early enough for the school bus. Although Michael is clearly bright, there is no reason for him to achieve because his parents reward him no matter what he does. His parents have clearly fallen into the wimpy parent trap, and now Michael is in real danger of failing at just about everything he does.

Limit setting is not an inflexible process. A component of limit setting is that children should always understand what the rules of your house are. Obviously the older the child, the more explicit the rules should be.

Wimpy Parent Excuses for Failing to Set Limits

"He doesn't always act this way, it's just that I let him have a chocolate bar earlier today. Chocolate always makes him hyper."

"She's not usually so whiny; she's just tired."

"What do you expect; he's all boy."

"I was exactly like her when I was a girl."

"She just isn't used to sharing her toys. That's why I buy one for each of them."

"He insists that I buy him a treat every time we go to the grocery store."

"I think that the red dye in some of those sugary drinks, like Hawaiian Punch, and the caffeine in soft drinks really make my kids hyper."

"I know I give in a lot, but I don't want my kids to grow up hating me."

"He's such a strong-willed child."

"I don't want to damage his self-esteem. After all, he's not really hurting anybody."

"Maybe if I were just a little more patient, I wouldn't get so aggravated all the time."

Rules and Consequences

I have learned over the years that when parents complain "These kids are driving me crazy," it usually means that these parents have lost control of their children. What is often missing in these families is a clear statement of family rules along with an equally clear statement of consequences for when the rules are broken. Sometimes the families I work with have never devised rules; other times they may have rules but not consequences. And in some families there is a notion of consequences, but they are so haphazardly applied that the kids often get away with doing their own thing.

Deciding What the Rules Should Be

Ask yourself this question: "How are these children driving me crazy?" The answer may be something like:

- They ignore my requests for cooperation, so I often wind up asking them to do something ten times.
- They don't hang up their pajamas or make their bed in the morning.
- They come and go from the dinner table when they feel like it.
- They put off doing their homework until I start screaming at them.

By examining your family life, you can pick out the major trouble spots and then make up a rule for each. You don't want to end up with dozens of rules. You want a handful of rules that will make a real difference if they are obeyed.

- Children are expected to cooperate with their parents by the second request.
- Beds must be made and clothes hung up each morning.
- No one leaves the dinner table without asking and receiving permission.
- Homework must be done after dinner.

Once you have decided on your rules, the next step is to

come up with consequences for breaking them that are logical and powerful. By logical I simply mean the punishment (consequence) should be connected to the rule and make sense. For example, if a child leaves the dinner table without being excused, your punishment might be that her dinnertime is now over and she is not allowed to eat until the next morning. (If you took her bicycle away from her instead, it would not be logical, because bike riding has no connection to eating.)

- **Rule:** Children are expected to cooperate with their parents by the second request.
  Punishment: If parents are disobeyed the result will be a loss of the privilege of normal bedtime. Each time this rule is broken, bedtime will be made earlier by fifteen minutes.
- **Rule:** Beds must be made and clothes hung up each morning.
  Punishment: If this is not done the child will be grounded in his room for one hour after school. During this time the child will make his bed and hang up his clothes. The child will not be allowed to join the family for dinner until the work is completed.
- **Rule:** Homework must be done after dinner to the satisfaction of the parents.
  Punishment: Watching television and general playtime will be suspended until homework is complete. The sooner the homework is completed in a satisfactory manner, the more time will be available for play.

The next step is for the parents to introduce their new rules and consequences to the children. This can be done in several ways: You can verbally inform the children. Or you can give each child a copy of the rules and consequences. Or you can put a copy on the refrigerator and review them with the children periodically. I suggest you do all these things. Tell the kids, give them copies of the rules, and post the new ones on the refrigerator with weekly verbal reminders about what the rules of the house are. Your children will probably not believe that this time you mean business, so expect to be tested. Children who are out of control have little confidence that their parents mean business when they set a limit.

Rules for All Seasons

I hear "My children are driving me crazy" throughout the year, but especially during the summer months. ("I can't wait for them to go back to school.") Many parents relax on enforcing rules because it is summer. But a home without rules is a home that most likely will be chaotic no matter the season. If summer is a hard time for you, then make up a set of summer rules and add consequences.

- Children can't take food out of the refrigerator and eat whenever they feel like it.
- Children can't leave jars of food out on the counter.
- Children can't leave the house without permission and disappear into the neighborhood.
- Bikes and toys must be put away at the end of the day.

I want to remind you that it is important to praise your children when they do follow the rules. It is a good idea to say something like this: "Since you have done such a great job with the rules this week, I have decided you have earned a weekend privilege of renting a video and making popcorn."

Rules and consequences work best when they are used in a family that makes time to have fun and shows affection.

Whenever you find yourself pulling your hair out over your children's antics, the chances are very good that your rules have become ineffective. If you are yelling and screaming and making threats, then you know you have to set up (or review) your system of rules and consequences.

I recently read a story about a mother who was sick and tired of having to nag her son. Every day she would nag, nag, nag her son to clean up his room, pick up his clothes, do his homework, and so on. She found herself sounding like a broken record. Then the idea came to her to make a record of all her nags. Using her own funds she had a compact disc made of the commands she was repeating. ("Make your bed" was repeated over and over again for thirty seconds.) She called her CD *I'll Say It Again*, and she is offering it for $11.95 to other parents. Personally I hope she doesn't sell any copies. You can sympathize with this mom, but this story is a perfect example of wimpy parenting. Can you imagine our parents nagging us over and over to be responsible? There would be serious consequences for disobeying our parents. Not so in the 1990s. Instead of making a CD, I would advise this mom, come up with consequences for not listening. When rules do not have consequences, there will be nagging.

Telling Kids What You Want so They Listen

All parents have to tell their children what to do. You are more likely to get cooperation from children if you give orders in a certain way.

When you want your children to do something, don't present what you want in the form of a question or favor. ("Don't you think it's time to go to bed now?" "Please do me a favor and clear the table.") When you give an order in the form of a question you are inviting the child to say no. And when you camouflage your order as the request for a favor, you are giving your child the idea that you're asking him to do something he shouldn't have to do.

When you give an order, be sure you mean what you say. Too many parents tell their children to do something and then do nothing when their child fails to cooperate. There is no better way to teach your children not to listen to you than to give an order, and then not follow through to make sure your child did what you asked.

Be sure you have your child's attention when you give an order. Shouting across the room while a child is watching television or is involved with a playmate often results in a parent's command being ignored. Walk up to your child and, while looking her in the eyes and/or touching her shoulder, tell her what you want. It is even OK to gently turn her face toward you before you speak or to ask her to repeat what you just asked her to do.

While in a restaurant one day, I watched as a six-year-old wandered away from the booth where his dad and sister were sitting. When Dad realized his son was bothering busy waitresses he said, "Billy, will you come over here?" This command disguised as a question went unanswered by Billy. This was followed by "Billy, did you hear me?" and then, "Billy, the waitress is going to get angry with you; now get over here," and finally, "Billy, I'm going to ask you one more time, and then you're in big trouble." By this time, the father had asked Billy to cooperate four separate times and on four separate occasions Billy had ignored his father. Each time Billy's recalcitrance was rewarded by his getting his own way. The frustrated father was actually teaching Billy how *not* to listen.

Again, when you give your children orders in the form of questions and when you don't back your orders up with action, you end up teaching your children that not listening pays off. This child should have been given a direct order ("Billy, come back to the table now") and then if he didn't listen he should have been escorted by his father back to the booth. If the child resisted or had a temper tantrum, he should have been punished later at home.

Stopping Disruptive Behavior Quickly

Parents often make a common mistake when their children are acting up. Let's say your child is getting on your nerves with some troublesome behavior and somehow you hope that behavior will just stop. It doesn't, and you find yourself losing your temper. You yell, scream, shout threats, and inevitably the situation turns into a big mess.

Parents need to understand that when they go crazy they are delivering this message: "I don't know what to do with you kids. You are just too much for me." When you go nuts, you are telling your kids that you are out of control because they are powerful and you are weak. Guess what? Some children get a charge out of driving their parents to the brink of insanity. For some stubborn, challenging kids this experience means they have won over the big person—Mommy or Daddy.

The solution is to move in on your child and stop awful behavior before you have lost your mind. Intervene and put a halt to what is going on while you are still calm and can appear powerful. With this approach you are building respect while maintaining your sanity.

When Your Child Misbehaves

When your child is misbehaving, should you ignore the behavior? Or should you stop it and correct your child? Wimpy parents have an especially hard time deciding what action to take. When your child misbehaves, ask yourself three questions:

- Is this behavior dangerous? If this behavior continues, is there a good chance my child will get hurt?
- Is this behavior bothering other people? Are other people being made uncomfortable by my child's behavior?
- Is this behavior undermining my authority? Am I teaching my child not to listen to me if I let him behave this way?

A mother recently wrote me with a problem:

While we were in a restaurant my four-year-old son left the table to play with his cars on the floor. The owner of the restaurant told us our son would have to return to the table. Was I wrong in letting my son play? He's only a little boy.

1. Is this behavior dangerous? The answer is yes. A waitress could have tripped over this little boy.

2. Is this behavior bothering other people? Since most little boys make engine noises as they play with their cars, the answer is yes. Also, other people in the restaurant probably do not like having kids on the floor next to their table.

3. Is this behavior undermining my authority? Yes, because this boy did not ask permission to leave the table. He just left. The parents are in charge of dinner and should determine when dinner is over and when he may leave the table.

Let's say you are in a restaurant and your child is pouting because he doesn't like the menu. At first you try to coax him out of the pouting, but what if he continues? Ask yourself the three questions. The pouting isn't dangerous. It isn't bothering other people, and it isn't undermining your authority. So just ignore the behavior. Don't become an audience for your child's pouting. "When you are ready to stop pouting we can talk and see what else there is for you to eat."

Knowing when to take action as a parent—and when to ignore troublesome behavior—can strengthen a parent's authority.

Catching Your Kids When They Are Good

In the olden days, parents rarely if ever went out of their way to reward good behavior. Kids were expected to behave. Only if you did something wrong did your parents have something to say in the form of a warning, a scolding, a spanking, or other punishment. Catching kids when they are good is a powerful strategy for teaching children how to behave. It is based on the belief that *behavior that is rewarded will be repeated.*

Wait until your child spontaneously produces some behavior you like or that you wish to see more of. Maybe it is being nicer to a sibling, or asking permission to leave the dinner table, or saying "thank you" or doing homework without being nagged. Reward the child for using that specific behavior by bringing her attention to what she just did. For example, you may have just finished an important phone call that had to do with your business. You have two young children, and when you get off the phone you say something like "I want to thank you. I really appreciate your not interrupting me while I was on the phone." In this statement you have made your kids aware of some specific behavior that they probably didn't consider very special. You have also given them a clue as to how they can please you again and win your attention. You don't need to reward your children every single time they use good behavior. Periodic reinforcement works better. If you reward your children every third time they don't interrupt while you are on the phone, they will try harder to repeat the good behavior that you have taken note of.

I was recently visiting friends who were building themselves a home on Little Cayman, a tiny Caribbean island in the Caymans. The area around the house under construction looked a little like a jungle. One afternoon we were all hot and sweaty and took a break for lunch. As we sat down on some logs to eat sandwiches we heard something crunch through the brush. The sound got louder and louder, and I almost expected a dinosaur to break through. Instead it was a big iguana. I jumped, and my friends just laughed and explained it was their pet iguana, who joined them every afternoon for lunch. I asked them how in the world they trained a wild iguana to be their pet. They explained that one day at noon this creature showed up, and they fed him. Now he is there every day at noon to join them.

Behavior that is rewarded is repeated. This law works for

iguanas, and it will work for kids. Pick one behavior that you would like see more of. Let's say you would like one of your children to show more appreciation for those times when you go out of your way to do something nice. So you wait for that particular good behavior to show up and reward it. There are many ways to verbally reward good behavior: "Thanks for being so thoughtful." "I'm really proud of you for appreciating what I just did." "You're such a good kid." "Here, let me give you a hug." You can find the words: "Super, way to go, you're special, outstanding, great, well done, you're a winner, dynamite, you're on target, I knew you could do it, awesome, marvelous, that's the best, you learned it right, I love you."

The next time you go to the aquarium to see dolphins or seals perform, just remember that these magnificent creatures learned to perform, not because someone spanked them or screamed at them, but because someone rewarded them when they did it right.

Kids need to know the right way to behave. Catching them when they are good lets them know they are on the right track, and helps them to stay on it.

Maintaining Your Authority in Public

Many parents undermine their authority by turning into wimpy parents when they are in supermarkets, malls, and restaurants. Children should not be allowed to get away with bad behavior out in public, but parents often feel that their children have them over a barrel, and they don't know how to respond to their kids when they misbehave. Consequently children have a lot of experience in public places not listening to their parents and getting away with it. The solution is to let the kids know ahead of time what you expect when you go out with them and what will happen if they do not listen to you. (This is all part of rules and consequences.) This could include: going home right away, being punished by an earlier bedtime, and/or being sent to time-out in the car or at home.

(If you choose to take a child to the car, you need to either sit in the car with your child or stand by the door. If you do the latter, roll the windows down so you can periodically inform your child that when he is calm you will both return to the store.)

Supermarkets and Malls

Some children turn every trip to the supermarket or the mall into a nightmare. These children need to be shown that this kind of behavior will no longer be tolerated. The first step is to choose a couple of times to go shopping when you don't really have to go! You want to set up a situation so you can quickly come home without inconveniencing yourself. As you approach the shopping area, inform your child that if he misbehaves you will take him right home and into his bedroom for a half hour. On the other hand, let him know that if all goes well, when the shopping is done there will be some small reward.

Since your child is probably used to getting his own way in public, the chances are good he will act out, and when you warn him to stop, he will not. (This is one time when you actually hope he will misbehave, because you are ready for him.) After a reasonable warning, announce: "You are now going right home and then to your room." Expect a temper tantrum, but take comfort in knowing that the temper tantrum is a signal that you are getting to him. When a child misbehaves and doesn't listen to his parents, he should be made to feel that he has done something wrong and there will be a punishment. After a few trips like this, your child should start behaving much better. This strategy is powerful in demonstrating to your child that you are in charge.

Restaurants

Some kids are truly awful in restaurants (as many of my scenarios show). The next time your child persistently misbehaves in a restaurant, let her know that if she doesn't stop, she will lose the privilege of going to a restaurant with the family the next time. Your child will probably not believe you and will continue to ruin your meal. The next time you plan to go out as a family to a restaurant, hire a sitter for the misbehaving child. (Try to choose someone who can handle a temper tantrum.) The child who has been driving you crazy in restaurants is informed that the family is going out but she has lost this privilege. It is not easy to leave a child behind, but chances are you will only have to do this once. (I'm always amazed at how sorry parents feel for their children even though they have repeatedly turned a family outing into a nightmare.)

A Friend's or Relative's House

Parents find it particularly embarrassing when their children act up in a relative's or friend's home. Kids seem instinctively to know they can take advantage in these circumstances. If your child has a pattern of not listening to you in someone else's home, I suggest you try this: Let your friend or relative know *before* the visit that you are working on getting your child to behave better. Inform the person that your child may act up and that you may have to put him in a time-out, either in one of the rooms of the house or in your car. (Remember, if you use the car you have to stand outside the car until the time-out is over.) When parents are honest like this, their friends and relatives usually respect what the parent is going through. Once a parent is no longer embarrassed, and has a strategy to follow, the child often learns that misbehavior does not pay. He understands that he will not get his way just because Mommy is afraid to make a fuss in Grandma's house.

CHAPTER 8

—◆◆◆—

Rewards and Appropriate Punishment

There are times when you will have to resort to a specific program of punishments to get a child under control. This is all part of reinforcing rules and consequences.

Time-Out Chair

The time-out chair works particularly well with the uncooperative child between the ages of two and ten. When your child ignores your requests by pretending she doesn't hear you, or if you find yourself repeating a request four or five times, place her in a chair located in a "boring" part of the house. (Translation: This should be a spot where she can't see TV, but where you can see her out of the corner of your eye.) At this age a five-minute time-out is about all you need. You may eventually have to increase the time to ten minutes. You might also want to use a kitchen timer to help your child get the idea of time and to teach her to wait for the bell to go off. Inform your child that the time starts when she begins to sit in the chair quietly without complaining or trying to carry on a conversation with you. (If she leaves the chair, she gets placed back in and the timer is reset.)

In about five minutes, return and let her know that she will be allowed out of the chair if she is ready to cooperate with you. If she agrees to do what you originally asked, then she is allowed to leave the chair. Once she complies with your request, praise her. If after five minutes she stubbornly refuses to comply with your request, let her know she has another five minutes in the chair. After the second five minutes are up, come back to the child. Usually by this point the youngster gets the message. She either cooperates or she spends a lot of boring time in a chair. In general, this is a fair and reasonable technique, which can be repeated several times in a day if necessary.

What's really important here is that in just a short time your youngster will come to know you mean business when you make a request. What is really effective about this technique is that the parent moves before losing her temper.

Time-Out Room

There are those times when children need help in regaining control of themselves. Sometimes they fly into a temper tantrum and just cannot back off, or they are superexcited and wild, and despite all of your reprimands they can't settle down. It is at these times that I recommend the time-out room—usually the child's bedroom. This time-out is *not* to be presented as a punishment. The time-out room, which works for children between the ages of three and twelve, is a place to regain control.

Let's say your youngster's temper is out of control. You may choose to ignore his behavior, but chances are it's going to get on your nerves. Before you lose your temper, inform your child that he is out of control and needs a time-out in his room. If he is unwilling you may even have to carry him. Once in the room, inform him that he has a ten-minute time-out to calm down and get control of himself. A lot of parents ask, "What kind of punishment is this? Everything he loves is in his room." Answer: It's not a punishment. The goal is for your child to calm down and change his behavior. If he starts playing with Legos or puts on a music tape, then fine. After the ten minutes, he can come out and rejoin the family.

What about the child who goes to his room and actually gets worse? Many children will go into their room and start crying even louder or shout insults in an effort to get you to lose your temper and give them negative attention. The wise parent ignores all the noise. At times like these you might even want to raise the volume of the TV or walk over to a part of the house where the yelling can't be heard.

If you need some reassurance, tell yourself that all that yelling and defiance is proof that you are getting through to your child. You are in charge, and he knows it. Right now he is finding out that he can't distract you from giving him a time-out. Don't lose your temper and say, "I'm going to go into his room and really give him something to cry about."

Discipline for the Child Who Won't Go to Time-Out

Some children will not go to a time-out willingly. A preschooler or young child can just be escorted, but older children could require a physical confrontation. These battles almost always seem to make things worse, and, more important, it puts the parent in the position of looking both powerless and nasty. In situations like this, I like the technique developed by family psychologist John Rosemond, who has a nationally syndicated parenting column. He recommends that you take privileges away from the child who refuses to go to his room for a time-out.

Rosemond's strategy involves listing all the various privileges your child has on different cards that are at least six inches long, since you are going to put them on display. For example, one card might say "watching television," and another card might say "going out to play." Anything your child likes can be labeled a privilege. Also make sure to label one card with the word "free" on it. Next you need to punch a hole in each card and hang up all the cards like clothes on a clothesline. This is important for little kids, but you can just leave the cards spread out on a table or cupboard for older kids to read. Explain to your child that when he or she refuses to go to a time-out there will be a loss of one or two privileges.

You are now ready to take action when your child refuses to go to time-out. Your child misbehaves and you send your youngster to time-out, but she refuses to go. Walk over to where all the privilege cards are on display, and take the one labeled "free." This card is really a warning card. If your child gets this card, this is the last time on this day she can disobey you about a time-out without losing one or more privileges. This strategy really inspires a child to cooperate with time-outs.

Behavior Charts

Another terrific way to provide feedback and discipline to young children is by using behavior charts.

Let's say you have a five-year-old girl who dawdles in the morning when she should be dressing. Every time you say no to her she gets into a real snit. She also hits her little brother several times a day. You could use a behavior chart to discourage these behaviors while encouraging more appropriate behavior. Young children love charts; they can earn colorful stickers and privileges for displaying good behavior.

Here's a chart I would use for the little girl I just described:

Behavior	Morning	Afternoon
Friendlier to brother		
Helpful to parents		
Dressing self		
Controlling temper		

Once you have developed a chart, the next step is to present it to your child in a positive way. Pick a time when your child is snuggling with you or otherwise feeling close, so you have her attention. Remind her how much you love her and how proud you are of all the things she has learned to do.

Introduce the notion that there are a few things she can improve on. Some of these are hard to do, so to make them more fun you're going to give her stickers and prizes when she does very well. By this time you should have your child's attention, and you can show her the chart and the special stickers you picked out.

Here's where a lot of parents mess up. They expect perfect behavior in all four areas in order for a child to win a prize. As a result, many children give up and lose interest in the chart. You want to make winning a prize very easy in the beginning to let her see how the chart works and to give her a taste of how much fun this can be. At first, look for relative improvement. If, for example, she is a little friendlier to her brother this morning, then she earns a sticker. Start off easy, but as each week goes by begin to expect more from her. She has to work harder each week to earn the same sticker.

Here's another tip. If your little girl had a perfect day, then she would have earned eight stickers, four stickers in the morning and four in the afternoon. But we want her to get a chance to start off with success, so we divide the number of stickers in a perfect day by one half. All she needs at first is four stickers to win her prize. The next week make it five stickers, and the week after make it six stickers.

Lots of parents worry about giving kids prizes. Isn't that bribery? Aren't we encouraging the expectation in children that every time you do something you are going to get something? My answer to both questions is no. If there is a trick to educating children, it is to capture their attention, excite them about what they are going to learn, and make the experience as much fun as possible. A kid could not care less about not slugging her little brother anymore. A parent can take these important but boring lessons and turn them into something a youngster is willing to apply herself to. With a behavior chart, you are starting a child off on an easy level, and each week expecting more and more from her in order to win a sticker and a prize. Offering a progressive challenge is different from a bribe: "Do this and I'll give you that." You are not giving your child stickers and prizes for every action—only for a limited number of behaviors. When these behaviors are fairly well mastered, you will stop providing stickers and prizes for them. And prizes should not be as significant as a new bike or doll. The prizes most often will be rewards involving nonmaterial things like an extra bedtime story or a bike ride or a walk after dinner.

Review

With a behavior chart you start off with a few choice behaviors that you want your child to improve on. Then you select stickers that you know your child will love. With the stickers in hand and a colorfully drawn chart, find a good moment to tell your child about your plans to make it more fun for him to be more grown-up. Then the chart goes up. Start off easy so he can't help but succeed. Change the prizes from week to week. After a few weeks you may notice that one or two behaviors are going really well. Take those two behaviors off the chart and put in two more you want your child to focus on. Once you take a behavior off the chart, be sure to provide praise and recognition periodically when your child continues to show that good behavior.

If you have other children, you may want to make a chart for them as well. There is always room for everybody to improve.

The Child Who Won't Take No for an Answer

Some children get into a pattern of just not being able to handle a "no." Mom or Dad says no, and the child launches into a variety of antics all designed to turn "no" into "yes." Dr. Thomas W. Phelan's approach to this problem—his "1-2-3 method"—is a simple training strategy that works very well with oppositional kids. Here is how it works:

Sit down with your kids at a time when they are likely to be receptive. Point out what you appreciate about each of them. Get their attention with legitimate praise so that when you get to the criticism the kids don't feel you hate everything about them. Let them know, however, that there is some behavior that is wrong and cannot be tolerated: From now on there will be only one no, and you expect them to listen. Explain the following: "If you fight my no, I'm going to hold up one finger and say 'This is one.' If you continue to give me a hard time, I will hold up two fingers and say 'This is two.' If you have not accepted my no by the count of two and continue to challenge my no, I will say 'This is three,' and you will need to take ten minutes in your room."

With this strategy you are giving your children two warnings followed by a consequence. The warnings are verbal and visual. At this point in the explanation your children may be looking at you like you have lost it. They also won't believe you will follow through and do what you say. Let's say it is twenty minutes before dinnertime and your child wants a Popsicle. A snack before dinner makes sense only to a child, so you say no. Your child starts to challenge you with "WHY?" Instead of trying to talk or persuade you simply say "That's one," and hold up a finger. If your child stops asking, that's great, but chances are he will now say something like "I promise I'll eat everything on my plate." You respond: "That's two," and hold up two fingers. Now your child is probably angry and will tell you how mean you are. Now you say "That's three; you have to take ten minutes out." Within a very short time your children will start responding to your no's in a different way.

The Job Card Grounding Program

Sometimes children need some strong medicine to counteract poor behavior. This strategy, for ages six to fourteen, relies on a philosophy related to basic training in the military: If you misbehave you "earn" extra work. If your children have slipped into a style of just not taking you seriously, the job card grounding program may work.

Sit down with your child and list ten jobs that need to be done regularly around the house. As you make your list be sure your child is physically capable of doing each job. Some examples: vacuuming, dusting, washing the car, sorting laundry.

Write down each job on a card with a description of what is required. By writing down a detailed description of what has to be done, you avoid arguing about whether the job has been done correctly. Once you have your job cards completed, place them into a bowl or jar, much as you would do if you were running a raffle.

Explain to your child that when a rule is broken, or if he is defiantly disobedient, he will have to pick one or two job cards from the jar. (The parent decides on how many cards are drawn depending on the seriousness of the behavior.) Your child now has one or two cards for jobs that he will have to complete as punishment.

Explain to your older child that if he refuses to complete the assigned work he will be grounded. Grounding means he is confined to his bedroom except for school and meals. No TV, no stereo, no friends over, no phone calls. He will not be grounded if he does the work. If he refuses the work then he is grounded until he decides to cooperate and get out of being grounded.

What if your child defies you and refuses the work and refuses to stay in his room? If this describes your family situation, then you have a much bigger problem. If you have been a wimpy parent over a long period, the result can be a kid who becomes impossible. If that is true then it is time to get professional help from a child psychologist.

The Child Who Listens Only to Dad

In general, children often respond to their fathers better than their moms for several reasons. One, dads are often not as exposed to the children, so they take their fathers' orders more seriously. Second, fathers tend to have deeper voices and just look bigger and more intimidating than moms. Third, fathers tend to talk less than mothers when they give an order. Somehow fathers give orders with a more no-nonsense delivery, while mothers tend to explain, persuade, and discuss.

If a mother is constantly taken advantage of by her children, who snap to attention for Dad, then chances are Mom has a problem asserting her authority. If kids have gotten into the habit of not listening to Mom, both Mom and Dad should have a meeting with the children. The children should be informed that if they disobey Mom, their punishment will double or triple that night when Dad gets home. This may sound like the old war cry, "Wait until your father comes home!" But this is different. It's not a threat that tells the kids Mom is not strong enough to deal with them and needs Dad. What I'm recommending has Dad's full cooperation; he explains to the kids how he and Mom have decided to handle disobedience. Now when the children disobey and refuse to go to time-out or be grounded, Mom simply says, "You can take your punishment now or expect a double punishment this evening."

Common Ways Children Try to Get Out of Punishment

Parents need to stand firm to make sure their children obey the rules. When you enforce these rules, you can be certain your children will try to manipulate you and plead with you to get you to change your mind. The fact that a punishment makes your child unhappy or frustrated does not make you a bad parent. But it helps wimpy parents to know ahead of time the many ways children have devised for making Mom and Dad give in and back down from punishment.

- **Crying.** Many children cry when the rules are enforced. Some even sob hysterically. Giving in to your child is a sure way of creating a perpetually sobbing monster— your child will cry every time you back up your rules. (Just hand him a tissue.)
- **Breath-holding.** This is a scary technique some children use. Most parents cave in when their child's face begins

to turn blue. Stay calm and don't rush to "rescue" your child. Experts say not to fall for this one, because nature will take over when your child has to breathe.

- **Threats.** Children often will try to threaten you into changing your mind. "I'm never going to love you anymore" and "I'm going to run away" or "You will be sorry" are fairly common. Some divorced parents are so upset at the thought of losing custody ("I want to go live with Daddy") that they rarely punish their children.

- **Making Mom and Dad feel guilty.** Children make many guilt-provoking statements to push their parents' buttons. "You're a mean mommy." "If you really loved me, you wouldn't do that." "You're not fair." "You love my sister more; you never punish her."

- **Begging for just one more chance.** Making a deal and/or begging for one more chance is very common. Again, if you give in, you sabotage your authority. You probably have already given your child one more chance—ten times over—so why fall for this one again?

Keep these strategies in mind and be prepared for your child to come up with new ways to get out of punishments. Children are very creative. One little boy insisted it wasn't him but his invisible friend Harvey who messed up his room. Another child regularly calls up her grandmother and gets her to intercede. Always remember that temporary unpopularity with your children is better than being stuck permanently in the wimpy parent trap.

CHAPTER 9

~∽∽~

Creating a Wimp-Free Environment

It's important to weave certain principles right into the daily fabric of your children's lives. Become the kind of parent who avoids the wimpy parent trap by following certain principles. Ask yourself the following questions:

Do your children know that you love them? When children are in love with their parents, they are motivated to be good. All the discipline strategies in the world will not work if your children do not feel loved. Play with your children; hug them and love them. Children by their nature want to win their parents' approval by impressing and pleasing them.

When I give parenting courses, I tell parents to go home and plan a fun family experience, or spend some private time with the one child in the family who is giving them the most trouble. You wouldn't believe the response I invariably get at the next class. Hands start waving in the air. Each parent who has taken my advice is excited: "I don't believe it; the kids are listening and behaving better." When we get away from the sheer mechanics of running the family and focus on the quality of the family relationships, children become more willing to learn and to behave.

Do you stay vigilant? Make sure when you state a rule or set a limit that you stay vigilant, expecting your child *not* to listen to you. Kids are great testers. You tell them not to do something and they will test you to find out if you really mean what you say. Each time a child disobeys and gets away with it, that child has learned another lesson that parents don't mean what they say. From time to time expect to restate what the rules of the household are and what the consequences are for breaking those rules. You cannot expect to set up a program of discipline and have it work without repairing and fine-tuning it from time to time.

Do you and your mate support each other as parents? Parents lose a tremendous amount of power when one parent remains silent while the other one plays disciplinarian. Typically, the silent partner is the father. Many children interpret their father's silence as meaning that whatever mother is yelling about really isn't that important. Children will begin to label their parents as the "good" parent and the "bad" one.

Disagreeing is one thing, but putting down the other parent is something else. ("Don't listen to your father. He doesn't know what he is talking about." "Your mother is just riding her broom today.") When parents are consistently in conflict, they sabotage each other's authority, and the children end up in charge. Parents need to compromise so they can work out a list of rules and consequences they can both believe in and enforce.

Do you look forward to mornings with your kids and dinner with them at the end of the day? If you dread a particular time of the day, it's probably because your children are misbehaving and you are responding in a wimpy way. If you find yourself feeling miserable, you should stop and consider: "The children are misbehaving and *I'm* unhappy. It should be the other way around." When children behave badly, there should always be consequences for them.

Does every member of your family pitch in and help out? Parents have to remind children constantly that life is a two-way street. There is no question that the ledger will not be equal: Parents do more for their children than children do in return. But all children should be expected to contribute to the running of the household, and when they don't, parents sometimes have to go on strike. If your kids are taking advantage of you, then say, "For the next week I'm not doing any-

---

The Child Who Leaves Things All Over

Many parents complain that children always clutter up the home once they return from school. Coats, jackets, sweaters, books, book bags, lunchboxes, and boots are everywhere and nagging rarely works.

Here's a strategy I learned from a mother who couldn't get her six kids to take her seriously about picking up after themselves. As she explains, "I just open up the cellar door and toss everything down the stairs into one giant pile. This doesn't have its full impact until the next morning. That's when I hear them all grumbling down in the basement trying to locate their coats and sneakers and books." Sometimes a parent has to take such a drastic action to show children she means what she says.

thing extra." You will have to explain that you have to feed and clothe them, but cooking their favorite dessert or driving them to the movies is a luxury—an extra.

(A word about housework: Moms have a tendency to be frustrated with the way kids do chores. So Mom ends up picking up the toys, hanging up the coats, setting the table because she can do it faster and better. This teaches children that if they do a poor job, they get "rewarded" by not having to do it.)

How to Have a Troubled Family

Let's pretend for some strange reason you came to me and said, "Dr. Condrell, how can I have an unhappy family life? What can I do to ensure the atmosphere will interfere with the effective raising of my children?" I would answer that if you want to mess up, do as many of the following on a consistent basis:

- Keep the television on for hours at a time. This interferes with family communication and closeness.
- Avoid active playtime together as a family. Fun together is the best medicine a family can have.
- Never sit down for a family conference to hear from everyone how they feel about the way things are going.
- Do not develop family traditions. Traditions that families build into their life give a family character and a special sparkle.
- If you are a dad, put your career first and then rationalize that you're doing it all for the kids so you can give them a good home.
- If you are a mom, stay home with the kids as much as

possible so you can get a good case of cabin fever. This will help you to turn into a nagging sergeant. Justify your behavior by feeling like a martyr. This will eventually make you unhappy, and your mood will affect the whole family.

- If you are a mom, try acting as if you really know best where the kids are concerned. Every time your husband tries his hand at parenting, find fault with him and criticize him in a demeaning manner.
- Don't entertain. Don't let the children have friends over. Friends and relationships outside the home add strength to the family.
- Never settle your differences as parents. In this way these arguments about how to handle the kids will come up over and over. You will have lots of opportunities to fight. This consistent parental disagreeing helps teach the children how to become expert manipulators.
- If you both work, try to find work shifts so that the two of you are hardly ever together in the house. Like two ships passing in the night, you will have no time together, except maybe the weekends, and by that time there will so much work to catch up on that there will be no time for the family.
- Become a housecleaning nut. You want a home so clean that when people walk in they will never guess that children live there. In this way all your energy will go into maintaining an immaculate home, leaving little energy or patience for the people who live there.
- Have very few meals together. Feed the kids before Dad comes home. The important thing is to skip over one of the best times for a family to work on being a family. If

you do manage to have dinner together, then use that time to solve problems. That will ensure indigestion.

- Do not treat each other with compassion, sensitivity, and caring. Make sure you don't model the type of behavior the kids can imitate to help them get along. In this way you will set a great example for the children to be self-centered, thoughtless, and demanding.
- Try to give very few compliments to the members of your family. Criticize and find faults.
- When you communicate with each other, don't think about what you are saying. You want a lot of name calling, threats, insults, and swearing.
- Don't forgive and forget. Hold on to grudges, and give your spouse the silent treatment. Don't talk things over.
- Do not teach the kids skills for chipping in and helping out around the house. This way they will miss having the chance to contribute to the well-being of the group.

If this sounds too much like how your family runs, it's time to make a change. Try the strategies listed below.

How to Nurture Your Family Life and Stay in Charge

- **Television.** TV doesn't have to subtract from family life if you actively manage household TV viewing. In fact, renting a video and building a family weekend evening around a movie can be a lot of fun. Television, however, must be controlled because all too often it operates like a pacifier or a baby-sitter for children and cuts into the time a family has to interact.

- **Family play time.** Families who play together stay together. Fun is probably the most underrated part of our mental health and our family life. We always include a certain amount of fun in therapeutic sessions with children, because fun promotes closeness and encourages family members to give to each other.

- **Family conferences.** The notion of regular family conferences feels contrived to many parents. Once you have tried it, you will see how natural it is for the whole family to sit down and discuss how things are going. As a parent, you are going to have to exercise some patience and not argue with your children once they begin to relate some of their dissatisfactions. You will have to learn how to create an atmosphere in which everyone feels comfortable speaking their minds. Try hard to listen to the feelings behind what is being said. Expect to hear three kinds of things: what everyone is pleased about, what some of the conflicts are between children, and some direct criticism of you as a parent. Don't interpret this as disrespect; you are to be complimented if your children trust you enough to face you with some of the things they don't like. You will be a better captain of your family ship if you have some idea of where you are going. Feedback helps keep your family on course.

- **Family traditions.** "We always go to Grandma's for Thanksgiving." "Christmas Eve is fun because we get together with the Brown family and go caroling." "I love the Fourth of July because we watch fireworks on the beach." These are traditions. A family that establishes a variety of traditions helps give their life a special, unique character and provides the members of the family with something to look forward to. Don't be afraid to change your traditions over time.

- **Entertaining.** I never cease to be amazed at the number of people who do not entertain or who do not encourage their children to socialize within the home. When you bring friends into your home you are rejuvenating yourself. By entertaining you are setting a good example for the children, showing them how to reach out to others and be friendly.

- **Dinnertime.** Dinner seems to be the only time in most homes when everyone can be together, but a lot of families even miss this time. Families need to make dinnertime a real priority in their lives. I have never seen a family work well when the father or other members read the paper or watch television during dinner. A family rule should be established: Newspapers and TV do not mix well with meals. If you are sensible enough to know the value of having dinner together, don't make the mistake of using dinnertime to solve problems or bring up controversial matters. Save all that for after dessert—and family conferences.

- **Compliments.** Studies have shown that troubled families have one major characteristic in common. They rarely, if ever, give compliments, but they do dish out criticism. Showing your appreciation through compliments lets others know you acknowledge what they are doing for you. When children and parents feel appreciated, self-esteem goes up, and their sense of belonging and security is strengthened.

Keep all the tips in this chapter in mind, and you won't make the mistake of taking your family life for granted. Those things we take for granted are very easy to lose.

SECTION III

———❦———

From Toddlers to Teenagers

INTRODUCTION

—⦿—

"Where has my baby gone?" I hear this question a lot. I hear it from parents when their babies become toddlers and again when their children become teenagers. The fact is that toddlers and teens have a lot in common. They are both in a state of rebellion that drives parents nuts. Toddlers are rebelling against being treated like a baby, and teens are rebelling against being treated like a child.

If he could, a toddler would say to Mom and Dad: "I'm sick and tired of just lying around being a baby. Now that I can run, walk, talk, and think, I'm going to make up for lost time." The teenager is literally saying, "I'm sick and tired of being treated like a little kid and being controlled by my parents. I want to stay up late at night, hang out in malls, drive a car, and maybe even smoke and drink." Is it any wonder that with each stage the parents feel a major loss? It's natural for a parent to feel rejected by a toddler or teen whose message is:

"I don't need you as much as I did. I want to do things my way for a change."

In both the toddler and teen stage, the child expresses an instinctive drive to be more in charge of himself. The toddler may respond to parental control with statements like "Me do it!" The teen responds to parental control with "You're ruining my life." Parents can easily end up feeling inadequate, because they don't know how to handle such challenging behavior and because their children so often seem like brats—just in smaller and larger sizes!

CHAPTER 10

How to Survive and
Enjoy Toddlers

Toddlers are filled with enthusiasm, energy, and a desire to do things their own way. They are lovable, but they present a terrific challenge to their parents.

When I listen to parents talk about their children, I often hear them say, "She was a little angel until she turned two." Toddlers can be a real puzzle for parents. One minute your toddler is an absolute joy, and the next you feel as if you're raising the world's next dictator or lunatic. The strangest question I ever got was from the parent of a toddler who asked, "Can a two-year-old be possessed?" Only a toddler could make a parent even think of asking a question like that.

When parents talk about the so-called Terrible Twos I hear two messages just beneath the surface. (Understand that the Terrible Twos often start as early as sixteen months, and they can stretch out until the age of three.) Once their child approaches age two, the parents begin to feel bad because they feel incompetent. When you put the Terrible Twos together with the parents' interpretation of their child's behavior as "bad" and their feeling that they are failing as parents, you have the basic formula for falling into the wimpy parent trap. It's crucial that parents don't take the normal behavior of this age—which is just naturally difficult—and build on it until they have created a well-developed brat.

Remind yourself that there is a purpose behind all the negative, oppositional, and difficult behavior. Your two-year-old's mission is to stop being your baby. Your toddler is intoxicated with his new powers and eager to be free and active. He wants to gain independence and to explore and exercise his new skills. Almost all parents of two-year-olds find themselves feeling frustrated and helpless. It just goes with the toddler territory.

Wimping Out with Toddlers

Watch out for the three dynamics that pull a parent into the wimpy parent trap:

- The parent feels at fault and guilty for the toddler's difficult behavior and loses confidence in his parenting skills.
- The parent is distressed to see the toddler upset when things do not go his way and gives in when the toddler cries or has a temper tantrum.
- The parent continues to cater to the toddler as if the toddler is still a baby requiring instant attention and gratification.

Help! What Am I Doing Wrong?

Toddlers worry parents when they bite, hit, spit, bang their heads, suck their thumbs, have temper tantrums, hardly eat anything, won't stay in bed, shout "NO!" and will not share. All this behavior is normal for toddlers.

The majority of calls I receive during my morning radio program are from parents of toddlers who are concerned about all of these behaviors. Most parents who call in assume they must be doing something wrong or maybe that something is wrong with their toddler. And they want a quick fix. Many parents expect their toddler to shape up after they scold, warn, or punish. In order for parents to worry less and to be more effective, they need to understand the toddler's nature.

The Nature of Toddlers

- Toddlers live by the principle of pleasure: If it feels good or if it is fun, they want to do it. (Why else would the sprinkler be there, if not for them to run through it?) Toddlers are easily tempted, and they will do what they want to do once their parent's back is turned. A toddler's need to have fun and to explore easily overrides his memory of the fit you had the last time he reached into the aquarium to grab a fish.
- Toddlers have no conscience, a concept that doesn't have meaning for a child until somewhere between the ages of five and seven. ("Mommy, why is it so bad if I take her toy? I like it better than mine!")
- Toddlers have little self-control. It doesn't help to scream, "I told you a million times not to touch that."

You can tell a toddler a million times, but if the forbidden activity feels good or is fun, chances are he will do it again.

- Toddlers have poor judgment. All your warnings, for example, about how dangerous the street is mean nothing. If his ball goes into the street, he will follow after it despite all your warnings. Toddlers don't yet have the capacity to reason, "If I go into the street, then I might get hit by a car." For the toddler, there is no if/then thinking. He is too young for this mental logic.
- Toddlers are negative. A toddler's favorite word is "no," and his favorite phrase is "I don't want to." They want to show their parents they can do whatever they want.
- Toddlers have hair-trigger tempers. Their developing personalities cannot handle much frustration, so they easily lose control. Parents often wonder if there is a way to prevent the frequent temper tantrums of toddlers. You can minimize them, but you can't prevent them until about age six or seven. It takes that long for a child to gain self-discipline, so your toddler will often go temporarily crazy when she is frustrated.

Temper Tantrums

Toddlers have temper tantrums because during babyhood everything went their way: If they cried they got picked up; if they were hungry they were fed; if they couldn't sleep they were rocked. That is just the natural way babies are treated. But toddlers have to practice patience and become accustomed to not having Mom and Dad meet every need on demand. This comes as quite a shock to toddlers who have come to expect constant adoration and instant gratification. When toddlers find that things aren't the way they used to be, they collapse into temper tantrums.

The basic rule for parents of toddlers is: Don't wimp out and give in to a child during a temper tantrum. Remember, when behavior is rewarded it is repeated. Instead of rewarding the behavior with your attention, wait to reward your child the moment he *stops* the tantrum. Ignore the child as much as possible during the tantrum. In this way you make it clear that during tantrums Mom and Dad act as if the child is not there!

If the tantrum proves too much for your nerves, then remove yourself—pick up a book, or even turn on the vacuum or listen to your Walkman. Instead of thinking "This kid is driving me crazy," tell yourself "I'm teaching him self-control and that he can't always have his way."

Toddlers have been known to bang their heads on the wall or the floor. Since head banging usually panics parents into giving the child attention, this can become a habit. If you have a little head-banger, set him down in his playpen where there is a soft pad. If he is too big for a playpen, then simply place a pillow under his head. The natural consequence of head banging is that it hurts.

Also, if a child starts trashing or throwing things during a tantrum, you will need to take action. You will need to restrain him while not lavishing a lot of attention. This can be tricky. I suggest that you pull your child toward you so that his back is up against your front. In this position you can wrap your arms aground him and hold his wrists down while wrapping your legs over his legs. Expect that your child might throw his head back to show his anger. Say to him in a soothing voice, "As soon as you get control of yourself, I'll let you go. Calm down." You do not want to lecture or talk too much; you are just trying to keep him from hurting himself and breaking things. The only message you repeat is that he needs to get control of himself before you let him go.

Discipline Strategies

Childproof the house. Parents often ask, "How do you discipline a toddler?" At this age, you mainly provide discipline by restructuring the environment. Childproofing is just one technique.

From the moment children are able to walk, they start getting into everything. If a home isn't set up right, parents are going to fail at keeping their little ones out of trouble and danger. Not only is this exhausting for the parent, but the child can be bombarded with too many reprimands.

Childproofing your home will minimize the trouble your child can get into. Plastic covers need to be put over the electrical outlets. (Poking things into holes is fun.) Plants may have to be removed because your child is enticed by the sight of mud. (Dirt is neat to eat.) Compact discs and tapes may have to be taken out of low cabinets and placed on higher shelves. A gate may have to be placed across the entrance of some rooms, to keep a toddler in or out.

You are doing all this so your child will not be buried under a deluge of no's. It is not easy when you're just two and you get yelled at all the time. A child who is hearing only one reprimand after another not only begins to feel something is wrong with him, but begins to turn off the parent who seems only devoted to ruining his good times.

Pick your battles. A normal toddler can run parents ragged, but you can introduce some discipline strategies between eighteen and thirty-six months that will help establish your authority. There is no way you can make an issue out of everything your toddler isn't doing correctly. You can't expect your toddler, who is at an early stage of development, to listen and behave like a college student. In order not to drive this little person—or yourself—crazy with rules, pick your battles carefully.

By picking your battles you are recognizing that there are just too many things to say no to with a toddler. A common mistake parents make is that they want to make every instance of misbehavior an issue, so the child doesn't turn into a brat. If you target the important issues and stick to them, your child is safe from brat-dom. You can't police your child all the time.

Make a list of all the battles you and your toddler routinely get into. Go down this list and see which ones you can let go of and which ones you definitely have to set a limit on. For example, you may decide not to make a big deal about the way she likes to dip her spaghetti into her milk. On the other hand, you may decide that she cannot take food into the family room. You may decide that jumping on the couch is OK since it is old, but throwing toys around the room is a definite no-no.

Expect to be actively involved. Toddlers need almost constant supervision, which means you will be interacting physically with your toddler. That may mean distracting your toddler from putting his toy into an electrical outlet, or it may mean taking him by the hand to lead him into the kitchen for dinner. Toddlers are not at the stage at which you can give an order and expect to get a cooperative response. You literally have to be hands-on with toddlers.

Take a toy away. Toddlers are famous for using toys in

ways they were never designed to be used. Sometimes a toy is misused so that it may be broken, or as a "weapon" that does damage to something in the house, like the dining-room table, or someone like a little sister. In such situations, it is wise to issue a warning, that if the behavior happens again the toy will be put away. Most likely, your toddler will not heed the warning, and then you will have to follow through and remove the toy. This may cause a temper tantrum, which you can ignore, or you can relocate the toddler to a part of the house where he can cry. When your toddler has calmed down you can reintroduce the toy with this advice: "Now play nice."

Thank your child for cooperating. Your attention is a powerful motivator for encouraging toddlers to behave. Let's say his little sister grabbed his toy and he didn't hit her. This is a good time to comment, "What a big boy you are! You didn't hit her when she took your toy."

Make a game out of it. A good teacher finds ways to make a lesson fun. Let's say you want your toddler to help pick up all the books she took off the shelf. You can't expect her to do this by herself, but you have a greater chance of success if you make a game out of it. Say something like "Let's play a cleanup game. I'll pick up the big books and you pick up the little books. Let's see how many books you can find and give Daddy."

You can adapt this game approach to many activities. Most toddlers love playing in the water during bathtime, but they hate to get out to be dried off. So approach your little one with a towel stretched out like a huge blanket: "Here I come; I'm going to get you, ready or not." With a lot of fanfare and fun, you grab your little one and wrap the towel around him and dry him off at the same time. Making something fun that isn't necessarily fun can be a great way to get a toddler to cooperate with your requests.

Avoiding Bedtime Hassles

It's not unusual for two-year-olds to resist going to bed and then later to wake up and insist on getting into their parents' bed. Wimpy parents really struggle with this challenge; they end up catering to the demands of their little

---

Toddlers and Timers

I have found that a kitchen timer can be a useful partner in teaching toddlers how to set limits.

- Timers can announce to children that bedtime has arrived. Children are told that when the timer goes off, it will be time to get ready for bed. In this way, parents are relieved of making this unpopular announcement. And for reasons I don't quite understand, most kids seem to accept the reality of bedtime when the timer does go off.
- Timers can be used to notify your children when you have to stop playing with them: "I have time to play with you now, but when the timer rings, I have to stop."
- Timers can be used to set deadlines for cleaning up and putting away toys. "If you get your toys put away before the bell rings, you can win an extra story tonight." In this way you can make a game out of cleaning up.
- Timers can be used to let your child know when a time-out is over. This solves the problem of the child who keeps asking "Can I come out now?"

---

one until they are almost unable to function because of sleep deprivation.

Not long ago I had a morning session with the parents of a toddler who came to me because they couldn't get their son to go to bed. These parents were both successful trial attorneys who stood before me tired, cranky, and sleep-deprived. I thought to myself, "Only a toddler could take two powerful attorneys and bring them to their knees."

Bedtime Strategies

Child psychologists typically look upon the toddler stage as a time when the toddler has to learn some important life lessons. One is to be able to tolerate separation from parents at bedtime. The second is to learn how to put herself to sleep.

At some point, you will decide that you are no longer going to take your toddler into bed with you. When you bite the bullet you may be "rewarded" with crying and temper tantrums. (Toddlers resist staying in their own beds because they enjoyed a tremendous amount of closeness with their parents when they were young, and they are not yet very good at calming themselves down at night so they can sleep.) Don't back down because you feel guilty or think you are doing something mean. That's a sure cue that you are on the road to wimpy-ness.

- Make sure you spend time enjoying your toddler throughout the day. In this way, not only will you have fun with your toddler, but at night you won't feel guilty that you need to spend more time with your child.
- Develop a bedtime ritual that makes bedtime as pleasant as possible. Maybe each night there can be bathtime fol-

lowed by "tickle time," and then it's juice and a story. The routine can be anything you want as long as it helps your child feel relaxed about bedtime.

- Do not rock your child to sleep in your arms while listening to music and then put her into her own bed. This seems like a logical routine, but when the toddler wakes in the middle of the night she will expect music and rocking in order to get back to sleep. Also don't let her fall asleep on the couch watching TV and then carry her to bed. Again, if she wakes up later in her bed she is going to expect TV in order to go back to sleep.

- When your toddler wakes up and cries, don't take him into your bed. If you do, you are teaching your child that if he just cries long enough or has temper tantrums he will get his way.

One Solution: The Family Bed

One controversial solution is to sleep with your child. Dr. William Sears, a California pediatrician, has written the book *Nighttime Parenting* to guide parents in using the family bed. The family bed is simply a large bed that will accommodate every member of the family, including the pet. You can push two queen-sized beds together or purchase plans that show you how to build your own family bed. Families who choose this route rarely have bedtime hassles with their toddlers. When friends question what you are doing, you can explain that family beds have always existed in other cultures such as China, Japan, and India. In some cities there are Family Bed Societies, which can offer support.

Breaking the Crying and Waking Pattern

If you live in an apartment building, you may want to inform your neighbors that they may hear some crying because you are teaching your toddler to stay in bed. Since you may not sleep much the first few nights, you might want to wait for a Friday evening, so you won't have to face work exhausted the next day.

- As soon as your child cries, wait three minutes before entering his room. Once you go into his room, quietly reassure him that he must sleep. Lay him back down and stroke his back a few times and leave. Do not pick him up or give him a bottle.
- If he continues to cry, wait five minutes; then go back into his room and do the same thing you did before.
- If he continues to cry, wait ten minutes before returning to his room.
- From this point on, go into your toddler's room every ten minutes until he falls asleep. The purpose of going in every ten minutes is to reassure him that you have not abandoned him and to repeat this message: It is time to go to sleep.

Some children will fall asleep within a half hour, while others may take hours. Each night keep track of the time it takes for your toddler to settle down. After the first couple of nights the time to settle down should decrease. Most children seem to learn from this approach within three to four nights.

Common Questions

Q: What if my toddler throws up?

A: Toddlers may throw up at night while they are having a temper tantrum. Many parents become very concerned with this and take their toddler to their bed. Just clean your toddler up with little fuss; then lay him back down and leave the room.

Q: What if my toddler wets or soils his diaper?

A: Go about changing his diaper, but don't give him a lot of attention.

Q: What if my toddler shares a room with a sibling?

A: Parents often give in to a toddler if she shares a room and wakes up her older sibling. Let the older child know what you are doing, and let the older child sleep someplace else in the house—like a couch in the family room or in a sleeping bag—for a few days.

Living with Toddlers

- **Expect to lose it!** Only a saint could live with a toddler and never scream, lose his temper, or cry with frustration.
- **Give yourself a break.** Do your toddler a favor and plan to be away from her periodically so you will not be so emotionally exhausted.
- **Remind yourself that this stage will pass.** Use this trying time to introduce your toddler to the concept that you are the boss. Start to develop rules and consequences, so that eventually you will have a more civilized child.

CHAPTER 11

—◦◦◦—

Staying in Charge of Your Teen

MOTHER: "You're not going to get your ears pierced again."

DAUGHTER: "It's my body and I can do what I want with it!"

MOTHER: "It may be your body, but this is my house, and as long as you live under my roof you're not having your ears double-pierced."

Welcome to adolescence. It's a time for parents to complain about their teenagers, and for teenagers to complain about their parents.

Parents complain:

"He has no purpose in life." "She won't lift a finger to help." "All he does is waste time." "She only cares about her friends." "I can't stand his room." "With all that makeup and her tight sweaters, she looks like a hooker." "I can't trust him anymore." "I have no control over him." "She seems to resent us so much." "He just throws his money away on that girlfriend of his." "I just know she's going to get pregnant, the way she sees him every night."

Teenagers complain:
"They treat me like a little kid." "I can never talk to them." "Mom thinks I'm having sex all the time." "I can never measure up to my dad's standards." "They are always butting in." "I have no freedom." "My mother wants to live my life for me." "It's always 'Clean your room,' 'Do your homework,' and 'Why don't you ever dress right?' "

Accept the fact that adolescence is a tough stage. Parents of younger children often brace themselves for this stage because they have heard so many war stories from the embattled parents of teens. Sometimes worried parents find their way to my office: "If he's not listening to us now at nine, what will we do when he's a teenager?" That's a very good question.

There is a key to unlocking the mystery of adolescence. Learn the purpose of adolescence. Understand what is appropriate behavior at this time of life. Finally, learn how your parenting style must be modified for this stage.

The Purpose of Adolescence

To understand what makes teenagers tick, you must never forget what's in their hearts throughout this stage. Every teenager has one major purpose in life, and that is to stop being a child. Teenagers want to stop needing their parents.

Some time ago, my former wife and my teenage daughter

went out shopping. These mother-daughter shopping trips usually worried me a bit since teenage daughters and their mothers are notorious for getting on each other's nerves because of their different tastes. They both returned home in a really rotten mood. My ex-wife thought it would be a wonderful idea to buy her daughter a new bedspread for her room. To my ex-wife's amazement, our daughter turned down her mother's offer for a new bedspread because she said it would be a waste of money. After all, she was a junior in high school. Next year she would be a senior, and then she would go off to college. As my ex-wife told me the story, I could see the tears in her eyes. The thought of losing a daughter hurt.

It's the job of every adolescent to stop depending on her parents. That's what our teenager was doing in turning down the new bedspread.

Since breaking away is not easy, teens put a lot of energy into it. Diplomacy and adolescence generally do not go together, so teenagers are very blunt in what they say. There's usually too much self-centeredness at this time of life for the average teenager to think much about the effect he is having on his parents.

The parent who doesn't understand the developmental need of teens to pull away will feel hurt, which can easily turn into anger that provokes the parent to fire back with sharp criticism of the teen's behavior. The situation is guaranteed to make the teen feel very much like a child again and have to come on even stronger. Just think how much easier it is now that you understand that the teenager is simply pulling away because he *has* to.

Pulling away, however, is not synonymous with "alienation," which means growing apart with bad feelings. Parents and teenagers can survive this stage of life without alienation.

In fact, watching your "baby" change into a young adult can be a joy.

Appropriate Teen Behavior

Many parents are not aware that there are great differences between age-appropriate behavior for a teenager and for a younger child. The differences, in fact, can be shocking. As a parent, you should know and anticipate the special ways a teenager behaves in an effort to grow up.

Rebellion

One of the ways teenagers stop being children is by rebelling against their parents. They do this because they have a terrific need to prove to themselves that they have a mind of their own. They need to establish themselves as individuals with their own feelings, values, tastes, and opinions.

Some time ago, I was talking to the mother of a teenage daughter who had been blind since birth. They had gone shopping together to buy the daughter a new dress. After searching the dress rack, the mother found a dress she thought was perfect.

"What color is it, Mom?"

"Red."

"I don't want it; I hate red."

The mother, not understanding her daughter's need to make her own choices, became sharply critical: "What do you mean, you don't like red? You don't even know what red is. You've never seen it." In a flash they were into a big conflict with each other. I never forgot this story, because it shows how all teenagers have the same need to have it their own way, for the sole purpose of having it their way.

This need to rebel seems to be programmed into each child to emerge during the teen years. Just as he had the need to explore as a toddler, the teen experiences the need to rebel. There was no way, short of tying him up, that you could have prevented him from crawling then. You have the same situation with your adolescent now.

Some parents mistakenly believe that if they raise their children "correctly" they will not rebel. But it is a psychological fact that if a teenager is going to be able to achieve an identity of his own, it is necessary for him to assert himself. Keep in mind, however, that rebelling is not the same thing as misbehaving.

- Certain teens are very immature. At the time of adolescence, when they should be interested in being less dependent and more grown-up, they may put all of their energy into being close to Mom and Dad.
- Sometimes teenagers do not rebel because they have been dominated all their lives by their parents. These teens have developed into submissive personalities. This is how they adapt to life with autocratic parents who continue to run their children's lives while dishing out very strong consequences for not pleasing Mom and Dad.

Understand that immature teens and dominated teens will all rebel someday; sooner or later, they must become independent.

Safe and Unsafe Ways to Rebel

Fortunately for parents, there are many safe ways for a teenager to show his independence. He can leave his room a mess for weeks on end. He can sleep half of Saturday, thereby encouraging his parents to believe that he is wasting his life away. He can hang around for hours with his friends at the mall. Then there are clothes. Every generation has access to fashions that their parents can't stand. A teen can choose hairstyles he knows his parents disapprove of.

Years ago the rage was for teens to get their ears pierced. Most parents went crazy at the idea that their daughters were going to have holes in their earlobes. As soon as this fad began to die down, parents were faced with a new challenge. Now their sons wanted an ear pierced and their daughters were asking to have their ears double-pierced. I think I spent a thousand hours in my office trying to help parents and teens deal with this one.

A new battleground had been established. Pierced ears were no longer something that would rattle the cage of most parents. Even seven- and eight-year-olds were getting their ears pierced. Now, of course, there's body piercing involving the nose, lips, navel, and other exotic body parts. And let's not forget tattooing.

Curfew is another area where some teens do battle. Don't expect your teen to come home exactly at the time you state. If you say 5:30, he will be home around 6:00. The wise parent builds in a grace period of about fifteen to forty-five minutes when setting a time to come home. This is a good way to keep yourself from going crazy trying to get your teen home at a specific time. Let your child know that if he is going to be late, you would appreciate a call.

Many teens are also very clever when it comes to selecting

companions that their parents don't approve of. Naturally the more parents complain about these companions, the more they will show up on the doorstep.

These are all examples of safe ways of rebelling because they do not involve sex, the use of drugs and alcohol, or extreme defiance, which can bring teens and parents considerable grief. You should be thankful if your teen has chosen to rebel in relatively safe ways.

Rejection

Resisting family activities is a major teen behavior. It is normal for teens to spend less and less time with their family in an effort to be independent. A common complaint I hear is: "Doctor, our daughter doesn't want to go out with us anymore." Some parents even bark at their teen: "What's the matter, aren't we good enough for you anymore?"

Don't insist that your teen accompany you on every family activity. It doesn't matter what other people think—Grandma will just have to do without her granddaughter this week.

You aren't being rejected because your teenager doesn't love you. Your teen is just practicing breaking away from his dependency on the family. She is trying to become psychologically independent. The trick is not to take it personally.

Put-downs

One way your teen can prove that he doesn't need you is to put you down for just about everything. By putting you down, your teen is convincing himself that you're not so great after all. If you're not so great, this reasoning goes, then he has a chance of having some smarts himself. So the era of your being the greatest is coming to an abrupt end. Suddenly your advice will be considered dumb: You will be criticized for the music you listen to, the clothes you wear. Your teen will accuse you of saying stupid things. Your skills, talents, and successes mean nothing to your teen. Some days your teen will make you wonder if you can do anything right.

Several years ago, I took my teenage daughter to a party. I insisted on walking her up to the door. Halfway up the walk my daughter turned to me and warned, "Now Dad, please don't say anything to embarrass me." There I was, a child psychologist, an expert in communications with years of experience in relating to families. Yet my own daughter was begging me not to embarrass her.

Baiting

You will not only be put down by your teen; your teen will also put you on. She will pull your leg, so to speak, just to see your reaction.

So some lazy afternoon your teenage daughter will wander in from school and say casually, "Hey, Mom, what would you do if I came home pregnant?" If you get upset she will have accomplished her mission. The more upset you become, the more proof she has that she is grown-up. After all, you would never have gotten that upset if you didn't think that she was mature enough to get pregnant. She's not such a little girl. You have confirmed that with your reaction.

Sons have their own way of baiting. After dinner one sixteen-year-old boy approached his father with the proposition that he and his buddies were planning to hitchhike to California this summer. If he had taken the bait, the father would have started raving at his son, the idiot, who would either die of thirst crossing the desert, or be run over by a semitruck. Before he knew it, they would be fighting, which of course would validate his son's feelings that he is a man—otherwise his father wouldn't have gotten so upset.

How should you respond when your teenager baits you? You have a better chance of staying in control now that you understand that teens bait their parents just to prove they are capable of doing grown-up things. Stay reasonably calm and engage your teen in conversations; ask questions and really listen to the answers. For example, you might ask your daughter, "Have you been wondering what would happen to your life if you got pregnant now?" Or you could question your son who wants to hitchhike, "Have any of your friends done that?" You want to show interest and explore what they are bringing up. You can still express your concerns as long as you don't lose your cool.

Omnipotence

Teens often feel all-powerful, all-knowing. They can do anything. Mature adults rarely feel omnipotent, because life has taught them humility.

Some time ago I was driving home alone from a party when I took a wrong turn. Unfortunately I was way out in the country and found myself on a narrow clay road in the wintertime. (A clay road in winter is the frozen equivalent of quicksand.) I was stuck in ooze that threatened to swallow my car. I worked my way to a farmhouse and called the friends I had just left. Within minutes they organized a rescue party made up of all the teenage boys who were at the house. Even though it was a freezing night, the boys all showed up without hats or gloves. They looked at my car stuck in this swamp and said, "No problem—we'll pick it up and carry it out." Even when I pointed out that the car weighed four thousand pounds they said, "No sweat." I was dealing with teens who were infected with omnipotence—they were deluded into feeling they could do anything. After several attempts to lift my car, reality finally set in, and they decided to tow me out.

Tell a teenager that he will catch cold walking to school in the snow wearing sneakers, and he will scoff. Tell a teenage girl that she might be attacked if she continues to hitchhike and she will look at you like you're overprotective nutty parents. These things just don't happen to teenagers.

Moods

Teenagers are very moody people. One minute they are bubbly and silly, and the next they are sitting in their rooms morose and morbid as if the world is destined to come to an end. The changes are lightning quick and so is the irritability. Just because your teen woke up with a smile is no insurance that by noon things won't be very different. Part of this is due to body chemistry, as they experience many growth changes. Everything is very intense. If you can stand it, listen to the music teens listen to—it's provocative and filled with themes of love and rejection and being free.

Try to ignore your teen's moods as much as possible. Don't react to each change with statements like "*Now* what's wrong with you?" Encourage him to talk about his feelings by being a good listener.

The Teen Who Refuses to Clean His Room

Teenagers typically have messy rooms. Since a messy room is one of those safe ways to rebel, I generally recommend that the preteen or teen can have his room just about any way he wants. But on Saturday it has to be cleaned, all clothes are put away, the room is dusted and vacuumed, and you can once again see the floor. Since you have given your kid a lot of freedom all week long regarding his room, you can make a rule about cleaning up on the weekend.

Instead of calling your teen a slob or making other comments about his character, I suggest you accept the responsibility for wanting the room clean. Say "I can't stand having a house with a room like this, and I want it cleaned every Saturday. Once the room is clean you are free to go out with your friends."

Announce that if the room isn't done by two P.M. on Saturday that you will clean the room yourself. This announcement usually strikes terror in the hearts of teens. If this doesn't work, just go into his room with a giant plastic garbage bag and put everything that is on the floor and on the bed into it. Then just tie up the bag and leave it on the middle of his bed. Expect outrage and indignation. Say, "I have been asking you for weeks to clean your room on Saturday. If you don't like the way I clean, I suggest you start taking care of your room yourself."

Adjusting Your Parenting Style

Nature plays a rotten trick on parents. As one father put it, "After fourteen years of learning how to be a father, I now have to start all over again, learning how to be a parent of an adolescent."

When our children were babies, much of our parenting involved using our authority and control: "Take that out of your mouth." "Don't put your finger in the socket." "Eat your vegetables." During the middle years of childhood we continued: "It's time to put your toys away." "You're not going outside without your coat." "No, you can't watch the late show on television."

But now, during adolescence, you can't exercise your authority all the time, because if a teenager feels dominated and controlled, he will only be inspired to fight you with all his heart. Parents need to be careful how they exercise their authority. Use it for the really big issues that will come up, like when you take the car keys away from your teen because he has alcohol on his breath. Don't waste it on daily petty issues that will leave your teen so hostile that he won't listen to you when the big problems come along.

You have to shift gears to become less bossy and act more as an advisor and negotiator. Let's suppose your fifteen-year-old daughter comes bounding through the front door all excited about some plans she and her girl friends have. "Guess what. Suzie, Karen, Barbara and myself are going to the mall for the day. Barb's mother is driving us at eleven. We're going to walk around, do some shopping, have dinner, and then walk over to the roller rink to skate until about seven P.M." The thought of your daughter roaming around a mall for hours and walking for about two miles to a roller-skating rink may strike you as just way too much for her age.

You have two ways to respond. You could come on real strong: "Are you crazy? Do you think for one minute I'm going to let you bum around a mall for a day and then walk along that highway for two miles? Over my dead body." Even though you might win, you would lose by creating a lot of resentment.

There is a better way. Keep your cool. Even though her request is out of line, it doesn't mean your response has to be. Put yourself in your daughter's shoes. Say "It sounds like you have planned a fun day, but we have to talk this over." During the discussion let your daughter know that you have a few concerns. You don't like her roaming around the mall for so many hours. And of course you don't like the idea of young girls out at night alone, walking along a busy highway. If she agrees to sit down with you, then you can begin to negotiate and compromise until you arrive at a reasonable plan. If not, she won't be able to go. Period.

Positive Approaches

- **Deal with their friends.** Friends fill in the gap left when teens separate from their parents. Teens are notoriously loyal to their buddies. Criticizing your teenager's friends outright is very risky. Avoid directly attacking your teen's friends. Teens are often drawn to friends just because they are different from what his family would approve of.

  Try not to limit your teen's use of the phone too much. Think of it this way: He's using the phone as a way to learn more about getting along with his peers.

- **Understand that all teens make mistakes.** It is amazing how parents panic at the thought of all the possible trouble their teenager can get into. There is no way your teen can settle into the right way to behave without first making mistakes. In fact, teens learn a great deal about life through making their own mistakes. Try not to bring up the past over and over. (If you keep replaying his mistake, your teen will just stop listening to you.) When your teen does goof, talk to him about it, if necessary withdraw a privilege for a while, and then give him another crack at it. Expect trouble so you won't go into shock every time something happens. Give your teen second chances.

- **Slow down the no's.** When our children were little, we often said no, only to think later that with a little bit of effort on our part we could have said yes. Our instinct is to make our life easier by saying no real fast. This habit can get to be a real pain during adolescence. Remember that each time your teen comes to you with a request, there may be parts of that request that are acceptable to you. Don't reject the whole idea just because of the unacceptable parts. Acknowledge that your teen's idea sounds like fun, so that he will feel that you are on his side. You want your teen to know that you are willing to negotiate.

- **Don't set alarm clocks.** Parents often have a terrible time keeping little children in their own beds. Most often they are up at the crack of dawn. Not teenagers. They love to sleep and they particularly love to sleep late on the weekends. Let them. If there are chores that need to be done, then make it clear to your teenager that these chores have to be completed before he can leave the house. You don't have to get him up at 9:30.

- **Don't make them feel small.** Teenagers put a lot of energy into trying to feel grown-up. They actually thank me when I miscalculate their age and guess they are one or two years older. Since they have such a strong aversion to being considered "little," you need to be careful of their feelings. The smart parent avoids references that make them feel like kids. Don't say things like: "Who do you think you are?" Or "You know you are only fourteen."

- **Watch your criticism.** It is so easy to find fault with teenagers that the temptation to criticize is very strong. Nag too much and he will avoid you like the plague. When you are about to criticize your teen's music or clothes, ask yourself, "Is he getting drunk? Is she stealing? Is he into drugs?" Knowing your teenager is not into self-destructive ways will give you the courage to hold back on excessive criticism.

- **Don't snoop.** Don't search her room when she is not around. Even if you are not sure what she has been up to lately, it's not your place to read her diary or do a search under the mattress. Snooping is sneaky and undermines trust. However, there may be times when you strongly suspect that your teen is into drugs or alcohol, and then you do need to do whatever you can to check up on her.

- **Don't run grounding into the ground.** When you do find it necessary to ground your teen, make sure it's for a brief period of time. If you make it indefinite or for too long, he will feel he is grounded forever.

- **Keep your house open.** You don't want your house to be off limits for teens. Let your teen know your door is open. Put up with the noise, the silliness, the raid on your refrigerator, and you will at least know what your teen is up to and who she is up to it with!

Overreacting to Adolescent Behavior

I will never forget one mom who didn't understand the nature of adolescence. She was fortunate to have a fairly compliant seventeen-year-old son. He maintained high grades, had a part-time job, and was rarely difficult. One day, in a moment of adolescent rebellion, he withdrew $500 from his savings account and bought a really first-class mountain bike. The mother immediately overreacted. In a flash, she concluded that he had defied her and clearly demonstrated that he didn't understand the value of money, and she decided he had to be punished. She went to the hardware store and purchased a six-foot length of chain similar to the strength used by tow trucks. With vengeance in her heart, she chained up her son's new bike so he couldn't use it. Of course, no teenager would stand for this. Even a basically nice kid would be inspired to increase his rebellion. Her son borrowed a welding torch from a friend and melted the chain. Mom upped the punishment by grounding him for the entire summer. The son responded by growing a ponytail, piercing his ear, and getting a tattoo. This mom did not understand teen behavior and turned a teen's natural need to rebel into an unnatural family war. It took months to achieve a cease-fire.

SECTION IV

⚬ᴥᵔᵔᴥ⚬

Dealing with Pesty Behavior

INTRODUCTION

—⁓—

Pesty behaviors are those annoying things that kids typically do, during the elementary school years, on a daily basis that drive most parents crazy. Fighting with siblings, whining, temper tantrums, resisting bedtime, lying, procrastination in getting ready for school, swearing, and talking back are just a few common examples.

These are the very behaviors that often make parents feel helpless and inadequate. To avoid being a wimpy parent you need to know specific strategies to handle these pesty behaviors effectively so they don't undermine your authority.

Many years ago, I was a camp counselor in a special camp for troubled and disturbed boys. The camp was run by the University of Michigan as a way of teaching students like myself how to change unacceptable behavior into appropriate behavior. Many of the students were overwhelmed because we just didn't know what to do with these delinquent boys. In the evening after the boys were asleep, our professors in child psychology would meet with us in a large conference room in the lower level of the main lodge. In a short time we began to call this the war room. Just as in a John Wayne war movie, we would meet to plan our strategies for the next day, to plan how we would deal with the "enemy." The enemy, of course, were little kids who were experts at undermining the authority of adults. It was in this war room that I learned two important lessons in winning the battle.

1. Never feel ashamed that there are times when you just don't know what to do with kids who are not behaving. It is the nature of children to dedicate themselves every day to getting what they want as long as it feels good and it is fun.

2. You usually get a second and third chance to correct pesty behavior. Kids don't just misbehave once and then move on to another misbehavior, never again to repeat what first drove us up a wall. A child who talks back today will talk back tomorrow. A child who refuses to get ready for school will do it again tomorrow morning. A child who rejects the dinner he's served and makes dinnertime an evening from hell can be counted on to be just as picky tomorrow. Kids do not easily give up pesty behaviors that get them attention and often get them their way. So as a parent you have a second and third and probably fourth chance to finally figure out solutions to put an end to these behaviors.

CHAPTER 12

⋙—✦—⋘

Sibling Rivalry

"Mommy, Mommy, he hit me!"

"I did not."

"Yes, you did."

"Robert, how many times have I told you not to hit your sister?"

"You always take her side," Robert screams as he storms off to his room. "You never listen to me! You love her more than me."

Slam. The walls shake as Robert bangs his door shut violently.

Sound familiar? Jealousy between sisters and brothers is the most common source of tension in the majority of families. Professionals like to label this problem "sibling rivalry." This simply means "competition." Sisters and brothers compete against one another in order to achieve a more favorable position in the eyes of their parents. The prize, of course, is more attention, more love, and a sense of greater status within the family as the most favored child. As the children see it, the name of the game is looking good in your parents' eyes while seeing to it that your brothers or sisters look really bad.

Sibling rivalry originates from every child's primitive need to be an only child. Children begin life as selfish, greedy little things. They want to have everything their way, and they think their parents are there for the sole purpose of catering to their every need and whim.

If you doubt this, observe eighteen-month-olds and two-year-olds. They can be pint-sized tyrants. They may as well have flashing signs hanging around their necks proclaiming: "ME," "ME," "ME." ME is No. 1. ME wants this. And guess what happens when little ME doesn't get what ME wants? A temper tantrum.

Children start off wanting their mothers all to themselves, but most soon learn that in this world they have to share. Mommy doesn't just belong to Robert. Mommy is married to Daddy, so Robert must learn that he has to share Mommy with Daddy. Then, when a little brother or sister arrives, Mommy has to be shared even more. Children struggle all their young lives with the difficult concept of sharing, and that's why jealousy and sibling rivalry can carry over into the adult years.

As a parent you can significantly minimize sibling rivalry. But if you take the wimpy path you can make it worse than it has to be. Again, if you identify the biggest mistakes you can make, you can avoid them.

How to Promote Sibling Rivalry

The wimpy way: Have your children close together. There may be some advantage to having children close together, but it makes it more difficult to manage sibling rivalry. If you have three children in diapers, you can almost be guaranteed a house filled with jealous children. There just isn't enough of Mom and Dad to go around to satisfy all these young children. Each child will find trying to learn how to share you very frustrating. (Also, an exhausted parent struggling with burnout is a good candidate for wimping out from the fatigue of dealing with sibling rivalry.)

The better way: If possible, space your children. Don't despair though if your children are fewer than three years apart in age. This doesn't mean you are stuck with a lot of fighting. It simply means you have more work cut out for you. By age three, a child begins to have friends in the neighborhood and a bit of a separate life away from home in nursery school. Therefore, the three-year-old can partially meet his or her needs outside the home. This gives the child a better chance to adjust to the changes a new baby brings into a home. In other words, the three-year-old is less likely to feel deprived because he has things going for him that don't involve Mommy.

The wimpy way: Make sure the kids have an uninvolved dad. A really stereotypical uninvolved husband can help create more jealousy. If Daddy doesn't help out at home, then Mommy is stuck with all the parenting. In a very short time the kids learn that all their fun and nurturance is going to be dispensed by one person: Mommy. This now makes her a bigger prize than ever before. The bigger the prize, the stiffer the competition.

The better way: Make sure Daddy is involved. Remind yourself that it takes two to make a baby, and it takes two parents to raise one. If Dad cops out on his parenting responsibilities, then Mom has to use her resources to convince him to take up his share. (See chapter 6.) Just make sure he is a real father, so your children will have more than enough love, nurturance, and fun. In addition, they will not turn to Mom for everything. Children with two parents feel more satisfied.

The wimpy way: Take your kids' good behavior for granted. When they do play together happily, say nothing. When they do share and enjoy one another, ignore them. Whatever you do, don't praise them. (Praise rewards children and makes them want to repeat the behavior that resulted in the reward.) By taking your children's positive actions for granted, you will have taken the critical step of not encouraging appropriate behavior.

The better way: Reward good behavior. Every animal trainer in the world knows the value of rewards. For some reason parents tend to ignore this basic law of nature. They often take good behavior for granted and get involved only when there is trouble.

Make a real effort, as we've discussed previously, to catch your children when they are good. Sometimes a few words of praise are enough. At other times a hug and a kiss gets the message across. Whatever you do, however, make certain that your children understand the connection between getting along with each other and being rewarded. Actually this is a fun thing to do. You will love the surprised expressions on your children's faces the first time you catch them being good with each other and praise them. "Boy, you kids are great." They may look at you half confused and shocked. ("I like the way you are all getting along! It's great when you have fun together.")

This is just one of the ways you can draw the connection in your children's heads between their getting along and getting a reward.

The wimpy way: Give your kids a lot of attention when they do fight. It may seem strange, but negative attention is indeed a reward and does cause behavior to be repeated, particularly when there's never any positive attention. Kids are often so greedy for attention that they eagerly seek either positive or negative attention. A mother's yelling, screaming, and struggling to settle a fight is a reward.

Here's how this works: The kids start fighting, and you dive in to get to the bottom of who did what to whom in order to settle the dispute. You immediately comfort the apparent victim and you chastise the villain, but then you begin to hear conflicting stories, and you're not really sure what happened. Like Sherlock Holmes, you try to get to the bottom and arrive at a fair solution. (It's a little like playing a living game of Clue: "It was your sister in the den hitting you with a phone.") It rarely works. Minutes have gone by, and the children are soaking up all the negative attention. When enough time passes, one child will end up feeling like the winner while the other child is, by default, the loser.

The better way: Reduce negative attention. This is what you should do when the kids start fighting. First, warn them to cool it. If they don't stop—and they probably won't—then say, "I can see that you children can't handle yourselves, so each of you go to your room for ten minutes. I'll call you when the ten minutes are up, and you can come back out and try getting along."

"But it wasn't my fault. He started it." To this you

respond, "I don't care whose fault it is. You kids have to learn to get along with each other. Now, go to your rooms and cool off, and in ten minutes you can try again."

With this approach you haven't been forced to take sides. One child doesn't win while the other loses. You haven't given your children negative attention, and most important, you have given your children a very significant message: You have to learn how to get along better, and if you don't you're going to lose some play time. The beauty of this approach is that it's basically so fair that it can be used one hundred times a day, if necessary, to get across the fact that they must work at getting along.

The wimpy way: Knock yourself out to be fair. If you are the type of parent who hates to see her children unhappy or distressed, you will probably do anything to appear to be fair. You will try to make everything even. For example, give all the children the same bedtime regardless of their age, so they can't complain that one is staying up while the other has to go to bed. When birthdays come around make sure the non-birthday kids feel compensated. Give them a gift or special attention. If you are shopping and one kid needs new sneakers, get them all new sneakers.

This emphasizes to your kids that you are a fair parent, which means all things will even out on a day-to-day basis. Unfortunately your children will pick up on this and never let you forget it. They will literally beat you over the head with cries of "It's not fair," to get you to lean over to their side.

The better way: Be fair in the long run. The attitude of consistent fairness gives children the mixed-up notion that everything is going to be equal each and every day. Life just isn't that way, but many parents create that expectation at home and then knock themselves out trying to live up to it.

One solution is to decide that over a period of time their treatment will be fairly equal, but not on a minute-to-minute basis. Teach your children early on that in the long run you will be fair, but even so there will be some differences. Robert, for example, is nine years old and can stay up later than his brother, Bill, who is only five. In turn, Bill at five years of age will have less work to do around the house than Robert since he's younger. Robert can go to a movie with his parents that Bill would find boring, and before the week is out Mom will do something alone with Bill.

When a parent operates in this manner, the children learn in time that they will each receive individual attention, that they won't be left out. However, parents must allow their children to "suffer" from time to time. When Robert has his birthday party, Bill probably will feel bad. It isn't much comfort that his birthday will eventually arrive. At this time, you can give Bill a supportive hug and say, "It isn't easy seeing your brother get a lot of attention and presents." Then he must be left to live with his unhappiness. It's a fact of life that this is Robert's special day, not his.

The wimpy way: Be in a miserable mood. A crabby, irritable, impatient mother is easily frustrated, overreacts, and has no time for fun with the kids. A mother's miserable mood can be contagious, and in a short time the entire atmosphere will be negative. A mother who doesn't take care of herself and ignores her own needs is most susceptible to such negative feelings. When kids become Mom's whole world, her mental health collapses and the fighting escalates.

The better way: Take care of yourself. For some women becoming a mother is such a powerful event that they become totally engrossed and immersed in their babies. That's how it should be initially. But by the time a baby is six to nine months old, Mom must recharge her personal batteries. She needs to make time for her husband, her friends, other interests. Mothers are givers, but they must also give to themselves. A mother with many interests will have better coping skills when the sibling rivalry games begin.

The wimpy way: Have a favorite child. Having a favorite child is a real promoter of jealousy. Because each child is unique, we can't help responding to them in different ways, and we can't always feel equally loving to each child. It's one thing to harbor some secret feelings of favoritism, but it's another to act this out in our parenting.

Parents can unwittingly promote jealousy among children by relating to a particular child without tuning in to the needs of the other children in the family. So if Daddy was a jock as a kid and one of his sons is especially interested in sports, then that dad, if he's not careful, could spend huge amounts of time with one son while leaving out the others. I have seen fathers favor one son over another to such an extent that the brothers ended up locked into a lifetime of competition.

The better way: Reach out to a "difficult" child. Understand that it's normal that one child may be easier to parent. Look for ways to help your more difficult child to blossom and feel successful. The more successful she feels, the easier she will be to live with on a daily basis. Ask for her ideas on how the two of you can have fun one-on-one. Periodically ask your partner how you are doing. The feedback can help you continue to be more balanced with all your children.

The wimpy way: Always relate to the kids as a group. Never spend time with each of them as individuals. In this way you will frustrate each child's need to feel special. By not spending separate private time, you will generate within them an even greater need for your attention. The result will be more fighting.

The better way: Teach that we are individuals as well as a family. One of the best things you can do to promote less fighting is to individualize your family. Spend some private time alone with each child. This is a wonderful way to enjoy your children, because they are often more of a pleasure to be with on a one-on-one basis. And an individual focus caters to each child's need to feel special.

Just fifteen or twenty minutes a week alone with each child will go a long way toward calming sibling rivalry. (Of course, if you can spend more time, so much the better.) Eventually, each child will accept the fact that his time with you will come. This is private time for you and your child to share and giggle, play and snuggle, and to plan activities while everyone else is locked out.

The best way: Teach respect. Help your children learn to respect each other's privacy. Have some basic rules such as: "Don't take anyone's clothes (or bike, or makeup) without asking permission." Or "Don't go inside your brother's room unless you have permission or have been invited."

If there is a big age span between the oldest and the youngest, then take steps to protect the older ones. They may have to put a lock on their stereo or place some of their prized possessions out of reach. Don't let little ones intrude on the older children when they have their friends over. Many times parents make a big mistake and urge the older children to make concessions: "Oh, he's only a little boy, let him be with you." Or "She's going to bed in an hour, just let her hang around. It won't kill you." Generally this attitude only helps to aggravate feelings of sibling rivalry. Older kids have a big emotional investment in not being treated like a baby. The presence of a younger sibling when company is around is often embarrassing.

The Challenge of the Only Child

Obviously, some children don't have sibling rivalry issues because they are only children. Being an only child, however, brings with it its own set of problems. Only children are also by definition first born children, and like most first-borns the sun rises and sets on them. Many parents of only children end up adoring and indulging their only child and wimping out on discipline because they are loathe to make their only child unhappy.

Somehow parents of only children seem more vulnerable to the fantasy that if they just love the child enough he will respond by cooperating and behaving. Essentially the parent of an only child reasons, "I'm good to you; therefore you should be good to me." Unfortunately when it comes to parenting, as we've seen, love is not enough; the parent of an only child needs to be sure to establish rules and a consistent program of discipline.

Parents of only children are prone to fall into the wimpy parent trap for several reasons:

- **"She's my only child; why shouldn't I indulge her?"** An only child doesn't have to learn how to share or to have to win over her parents' attention—she basks in the limelight all by herself. Just because you can afford to, doesn't mean you should shower an only child with all manner of extras. Otherwise your only child will have an exaggerated idea of her importance and her specialness.

- **The Three Musketeers syndrome.** In most families the children know that they are children and that their parents have a life beyond parenting. The only child is prone to thinking of himself as one of the gang—an equal member with his parents. It's not uncommon for an only to believe he gets a vote and is part of a triumvirate that makes decisions. Onlies also have trouble taking instructions, or orders, when they have been made to feel like miniature adults. Only children love to know everything that is going on with their parents and often wind up being little companions. Parents of only children should definitely schedule adult time apart from their child.

- **Wimping out with overprotectiveness.** Parents really put their metaphorical eggs in one basket— they bask too much in the accomplishments of their only child. They tend to have real problems letting their only child fail or mess up. It is easy for parents of only children to be overprotective, which can result in a child's being too dependent on his parents.

CHAPTER 13

Taking Charge of Bedtime

Bedtime problems are a real concern for many parents. It's one of the topics I advise people about the most on my call-in radio program. People react strongly when I talk about how young children need to learn to quiet themselves down at night in order to go to sleep, and that children need to learn how to tolerate separation so they can be alone in their own beds. Some parents believe that a child's place is with his mother whenever he wants to be there. Another group of parents believe in what they call "the family bed." (See chapter 10.)

My position is that parents should not be sleeping with their children and inviting them into their bed until they have learned how to handle bedtime. Otherwise, they will be in your bed all the time. Once children can manage themselves at night, an occasional evening with Mom and Dad is fine. Problems begin when parents reverse this procedure. They enjoy having their children with them, and then suddenly one day say, "OK, it's time to be a big girl and stay in your own bed." The child thinks, "I'm not giving up sleeping in my parents' bed. Mom is out of her mind if she thinks I want to be in a dark old room all by myself. No way."

When I talk about bedtime problems, I'm talking about healthy kids who are resisting the idea of winding down, separating from the family to be alone, and finally going to sleep.

- Bedtime problems commonly occur between the ages of eighteen and thirty months—around the time of the "terrible twos" when the toddler is rebellious and stubborn about having his own way. Children under three haven't mastered the idea that when Mom and Dad are out of sight they are not "all gone."
- Normal bedtime problems can develop into serious ones. I have been consulted by many parents who have ten-, eleven-, and twelve-year-olds who still refuse to sleep in their own rooms and bunk with Mom and Dad every night.
- Children differ in how much sleep they require. Your child may be one of those youngsters who doesn't need much sleep. They also vary in how soundly they sleep.
- Parents generally give in to the crying and screaming of their youngster, which just convinces the small child that making a real fuss gets her attention. New parents, who worry that they are going to harm the baby, give in quickly; they often become frightened by their baby's crying and rush in to fuss over their child.

Straight from the Source

The following letters reveal a great deal about bedtime problems:

I have an eighteen-month-old girl who was a perfect angel until five weeks ago. Suddenly she started to refuse to be alone in her bed at night. She fusses and cries every time I leave the room. She crawls out of her crib if I leave her so I can't even let her cry it out. She finally falls asleep around 8:00 at night, but I have to be holding her in my arms. Then around 10:00 she wakes up again and starts all over. When I rock her she falls back to sleep, but as soon as I go to lay her down in her bed, she starts crying again. The last couple of nights I have taken her out of her bed and I lay down with her in the family room. She seems to love this and goes right to sleep. There are nights when not only will she wake up at 10:00 P.M. but also at 3:00 A.M. or 4:00 A.M. I usually lie on the floor with her in the family room, and she goes back to sleep. She has a full-size crib, but refuses to fall asleep in it. I can't take much more.

I'm writing about my thirteen-month-old daughter who has never gotten into a pattern of sleeping through the night. Sometimes she does, but most of the time she doesn't. Some friends have told us to feed her just before she goes to bed, but this hasn't helped. Our pediatrician has told us to let her cry. Well, after a half hour of crying we couldn't take it anymore. We brought her into bed with us after changing her and giving her juice and she played and jumped around. Recently we let her cry for one and a half hours. She was so worked up she had a bowel movement. There have been times when we have let her cry only to find out she's teething or has thrown up or had a fever. Then for weeks after, we would get up the minute she lets out a peep. At this point our routine is: When she cries we get up within five minutes and give her juice, bring her in the living room, and change her and stay up for about fifteen minutes. She gets up three or four nights in a row. I am an expectant mother and would appreciate any suggestions you have.

We have quite a problem with our three-and-a-half year-old son. He refuses to go to bed alone. Either my wife or I have to go to sleep with him. So every night we go through the same thing of lying down with him so he will fall asleep. It's been going on for nine months, ever since we brought our new baby home from the hospital. We get up from his bed after he is asleep, and he is quiet until about four or five in the morning, then he gets up and comes into our bedroom and snuggles between my wife and me. Help!!

Let's analyze these letters. Below is an assortment of statements I have extracted from them:

- "I have to be holding her in my arms for her to sleep."
- "When I rock her she falls back to sleep."
- "I have taken her out of her bed and laid her down in the family room. She seems to love this and goes right back to sleep."
- "I usually lie on the floor with her and she goes back to sleep."
- "We brought her into bed with us after changing her and giving her juice and she played."
- "We get up the minute she lets out a peep."
- "We bring her in the living room, change her, and stay up for about fifteen minutes."
- "Either my wife or I have to sleep with him."

- "Every night we go through the same routine of lying down with him so he will sleep."
- "He gets up and comes into our bedroom and snuggles between my wife and me."

All of these children are getting extras at night. They are being held and rocked, they are having juice, they are getting out of their bedrooms. They get to play and they have attention in the middle of the night. These parents are all worried and feel they have to do something. It's this doing "something" that kids want at night more than anything.

Common Mistakes that Will Keep Kids Up at Night

- Make your home superquiet when your child is still an infant and is sleeping. Check every possible source of noise and put an end to it. Let the neighbors outside know that they have to stop playing basketball because it's your baby's naptime. Do not run the vacuum cleaner. In this way your baby will never learn to develop tolerance for noises.
- Get in the habit of lying down with your youngster each evening to help him fall asleep. Once he is asleep, sneak out of his room so that he is not awakened. Setting up this pattern early will keep him from facing the reality of having to go to sleep on his own. This approach fools you into thinking bedtime is really working out successfully. What you are really doing is delaying the moment of truth when your child will finally be faced with having to be on his own at bedtime.

- Let your young child fall asleep in your bed because she doesn't like her own room. When she is asleep, move her to her bedroom. This is one more approach that distorts the whole bedtime reality and keeps a youngster from learning how to handle bedtime.
- When your child awakes in the middle of the evening and cries, go to him to see what's up. Here is the most important part: Make these visits a pleasurable experience. Talk with your child, play with him a little, fuss with him, and maybe rock him for a while. The more interesting and the more fun you make your checkup, the more he is going to want you to stay.
- Bring your youngster into your bed at night whenever she wakes up. I assure you that in no time at all she will be waking up with greater frequency in order to have the pleasure of your company.
- Discourage your child from becoming attached to a "blanky" or to a favorite stuffed animal. These transitional objects become substitutes for Mommy or Daddy when they aren't there. A child who can hug a blanky at night has the satisfaction of feeling as if his parents are close. Transitional objects serve the purpose of helping young children tolerate separations.
- Make sure that your child doesn't see you leave the house when you and your mate go out for an evening, leaving a baby-sitter in charge. Parents often do this because they do not want their little one to get upset knowing that Mom and Dad have left for a while. But young children have to learn to tolerate separation from their parents when they leave to go places. If children learn to do this, they are in a better position at night to separate from Mom and Dad and go to bed.

- Do not ever leave your child with anyone but family. When you leave your child only with members of the family, you are not truly giving your child the chance to learn how to separate. Family is family, and it's almost like being with Mom and Dad.
- Avoid any bedtime ritual, that is, a routine that you perform at night to help make bedtime a positive experience. This way you have made absolutely no effort to make bedtime a more attractive experience for your child.
- The father should convince the mother that any bedtime problem is her problem, not his. After all, she is the mother, and he has to go to work tomorrow. A mother who buys this is going to find herself caught between her child and her husband. Most likely she will end up making every effort to keep the kid quiet so Dad can get his sleep and not get on Mom's case.

The Right Things to Do

- Help your child become accustomed to noise by having a normal, noisy household when he naps and sleeps.
- Do not lie down with your child until she falls asleep and then tiptoe out. If you want to lie down for a few minutes, make sure to leave before she has fallen asleep.
- Do not use your own bed as a pacifier and then carry him to his room while he is asleep.
- If your child cries at night, look in on her only once, and make it a matter-of-fact checkup visit with no frills. Your brief visit should not be a time of warm fuzzies, tickling, and playing.

- Forget bringing your child into your bed unless he is really sick.
- Encourage your child's attachment to a "blanky" or a favorite stuffed animal.
- Let your child see you go out the door when you're leaving her with a baby-sitter.
- Rely on sitters other than close family members.
- Have a special bedtime routine. You and your child can set the kitchen timer together. When the bell goes off it is bedtime. This is a little game that often takes the sting out of someone announcing, "OK, it's bedtime." Then comes the bath. (And whatever other "games" you set up, such as a drying game.) This is followed by a drink, a story, and then being tucked in.
- Enjoy your child during the day so that you don't feel compelled to owe him time when he cries at night.
- Make sure bedtime problems are handled by both parents.

Dealing with Common Bedtime Problems

Despite your best efforts, you may still have bedtime problems with your children.

Q: What about the child who crawls out of her crib?

A: Some children have the agility of a monkey and nothing can keep them in their cribs at night. Parents have found it helpful to place a safe, approved gate at the doorway of the child's bedroom so she cannot leave her room when she gets up. Make the bedroom as childproof as possible. Your goal is to keep your youngster in her room without repeatedly catering to her in the middle of the night.

Q: What about the older child who leaves his bed?

A: Firmly return the youngster to his bed with a warning that if he leaves his room again, you will have to close the door. Typically this warning is ignored the first few times a youngster hears it. Return the youngster to his bed; leave a closet light or night-light on; close the door and hold it shut. Most young children hate the door being shut and will immediately try to open it. Hold it shut for about five minutes, and ignore his yelling and pulling. Don't talk to him. After about five minutes, release your hold on the door and walk in. Offer your child another chance. You tell him in a no-nonsense way that if he stays in his bed the door will stay open. Most kids think this is a pretty good deal and will cooperate. A few kids will start up again, and you will have to repeat this routine. Most parents are surprised how well this works. It shows a persistent child that you mean business and that you are not going to get into any of his bedtime games.

Q: What about the child who sneaks into your room at night and stays in your bed until morning?

A: Parents often tell me they didn't hear the child come in. Place a suitcase or some object against your bedroom door at night. That way the moment your little one tries to sneak in, he will make a banging noise, which will wake you up. Then you can take him back to his room. When you return to your room, set up the "alarm system" again.

Q: What about the child who can go on crying and complaining for what seems like forever?

A: Most parents expect to solve the problems with their very persistent children in an hour, or in an evening or two. It doesn't work that way. If you have a very persistent child, you must have more realistic expectations. Most established bedtime problems can take up to a couple of weeks to run their course. To help you keep from becoming discouraged, I suggest that you begin to record the time that your child complains and cries each evening. You will notice that during the first couple of evenings he will actually cry for a longer period of time. Since crying has always worked in the past, he just can't believe that it won't work again, so he is going to try extra hard. After a couple of evenings you should record the time decreasing, because your child will be getting the message that you mean what you say. It is time for sleep. (See chapter 10 for more strategies.)

CHAPTER 14

—✦—

Talking Back

It's not uncommon today to encounter children who speak their mind no matter what they have to say. Young children must first learn to respect authority before they learn that sometimes authority does need to be questioned. As a result we have many more little ones running around saying: "I don't have to listen to you"; "You're not my boss"; "You can't make me"; "I don't have to"; and even "Shut up."

Many children receive this early training in talking back and also have parents who not only display disrespectful behavior to other adults, but do not take the time to teach their children how to be respectful. And then to ensure disrespect we plunk them in front of the television without any supervision, and allow them to soak up the vulgarity of *Beavis and Butt-head*. I recall one sitcom in which a widowed grandmother was living temporarily in her married son's home. The grandmother started dating and then the seven-year-old granddaughter asked, "Mommy, is Grandma a slut?" The soundtrack provided squeals of laughter for this "cute" line. Children all over the country got another lesson that saying disrespectful, hurtful things to adults is really quite funny.

Talking back occurs when a child gives a parent an answer that is defiant and disrespectful. ("Says who?" "I don't have to listen to you.") When parents say a child is mouthy or wise, they are almost always referring to the problem of talking back.

- A child who is into a pattern of talking back is also challenging his parents' authority.
- Talking back is rude and inappropriate behavior. Children who talk back to their parents give other adults a bad impression—of themselves and also of their parents.
- A child who talks back to parents will most likely generalize this disrespectful behavior to other authority figures such as teachers and neighbors. (This is not always true. As one smart child told his mom, "Oh, don't worry. I wouldn't dare talk like this at school.")
- A child who is into a pattern of talking back is a child who has learned to be verbally abusive when frustrated. A child who mistreats others with his mouth is going to create all sorts of problems for himself as he relates to others.

Some children talk back more than others. Sooner or later all children talk back. Very young children have yet to learn how to handle themselves when they are angry and they usually lash out verbally. It is normal for children to test their parents by talking back. Don't fall into a wimpy response and fail this test. Although it may be normal for children to experiment with talking back, it is not advisable to allow a child to settle into talking back as a coping strategy.

Some children are slow to learn that talking back is unacceptable behavior because it works for them. These children end up winning by getting their way. As we've seen, whenever a child receives a payoff after acting offensively, parents can expect the behavior to resurface again and again.

Dealing with Talking Back

Introduce your child to the rule of respect. If your child is starting to talk back to you, and you have not had much success in discouraging this behavior, then make the following announcement:

"There will be a new family rule, the rule of respect. That means that we don't mistreat others with our mouths. Talking back is unacceptable because it is rude and disrespectful." (This rule can be introduced to children as young as four, and works up until the adolescent years.)

Explain that whenever someone talks back, he will be reminded that he has just broken the rule. You should praise your child whenever he can self-correct after a warning. If the talking back continues, then you must follow through with a consequence.

Possible penalties are:

- Going to bed fifteen minutes earlier for every talking back event
- Being grounded or sent to his room for fifteen minutes immediately following the talking back
- Losing a privilege, such as television time

Use a behavior chart to teach your child not to talk back. Explain that for the next few weeks she is going to be rated on how successful she can be in curbing her urge to talk back. You will put up a chart that will be divided into morning, after school, and evening. At the end of each day you will look at the chart and see how many times she has talked back. If she has shown an improvement, then she will have all of her privileges that evening; if it has been a poor day, then she will lose privileges.

As previously noted, when you begin using a behavior chart, you want to look for improvement. Then, as the days progress, you are going to expect more and more from your child in order for a day or week to qualify as a good one. And by all means continue to praise your child when you catch her being upset but not resorting to talking back.

When you affect a child's standard of living, you end up motivating her to work on some specific behavior she may otherwise have had little interest in changing. You might even go one step further by increasing the motivation with the promise of a weekend privilege for a really successful week.

Use a code word to tell your child to cool it. Introduce the idea of a code word that signals to your child that she has just talked back and needs to rethink what she has said. Children often love the idea of choosing the code word; once the word has been agreed upon, the parent uses it to signal the child that he needs to correct himself. (For one child the "word" was really a snap of the fingers to "snap" her out of the bad behavior.) Using a code word is often a good way to help a child catch herself and self-correct.

Some parents will read these three solutions and say, "My parents never did stuff like that. When we talked back, we got a slap across the mouth or pepper in our mouths or our mouths washed out with soap." Your goal as a parent is to teach your child social skills—how to behave in a sensitive and appropriate way. If we abuse our children with slaps or pepper or soap, we undermine our ultimate goal of teaching kindness to others.

Constant Debating

Some children get into a pattern of turning every request into a debate. Whether the request is to clear the dinner table or do homework or practice the piano or pick up toys, the argumentative child launches into a debate about why he doesn't have to. Some children are very stubborn and must have the last word. Often parents begin to feel as if they are living with a zealous attorney who needs to argue endlessly. All too often the parents respond by arguing back, trying to persuade the child to cooperate. What results is one power struggle after another, which usually ends up with the parents giving up; maybe the child even finally cooperates, but only after the household has been turned into an emotional disaster area.

I recommend another strategy devised by John Rosemond. The parent should refuse to get into a debate with the arguing child. Instead of trying to one-up the child with a better argument, the parent simply walks away. At first glance this looks like wimping out, but actually walking away from a child who loves power struggles is the first step toward turning things around. The child may initially feel that he has won, but he finds out differently when the parent follows up the incident with a punishment for disobeying. For example, the parent may announce that bedtime is moved up an hour from nine to eight o'clock. The shocked child finds that he is now in bed an hour earlier for not listening. Or maybe the child asks Mom for a favor during the day; "Mom, it's time for me go to Billy's house to play; can you drive me over?" The mother responds, "You have lost the privilege of going to Billy's house, and besides I am in no mood to do you any favors after the way you disobeyed me." Through this disciplinary strategy, the child learns in a very short time that when a parent walks away in silence from a disrespectful, arguing child, there will still be a punishment.

Parents can follow this "say no more and lower the boom" approach by offering an incentive for cooperative behavior. After about a week of using this strategy you can say, "I have decided that you can earn a weekend privilege if you make a real effort to be more cooperative and cut back on all this arguing." The parent can explore some "grown-up" privileges that might inspire the child to try harder. (Using the phrase "grown-up" to label their improved behavior is a kind of reward by itself.) The reward may be staying up later on the weekend or watching a video complete with pizza or whatever inspires the child to try to improve. Sometimes pairing a punishment program with a reward incentive can be powerful in guiding children to behave better.

Talking Back As a Signal

There are times when talking back is the signal to a parent that the relationship is in trouble. Most kids talk back because they are upset with a particular situation or frustrated with some limit a parent has mandated. But some children who talk back are genuinely unhappy at home. Often we are too close to our family situations to be objective, and it can help to get the opinions and observations of others who know your child. First talk with his teacher for some feedback on what might be going on in his life. The views of a good adult friend might also be helpful. Then find a good time to sit down with your child for a heart-to-heart talk. Often adults see no reason for a child to be unhappy, but children are looking at the world with different eyes and put things together in truly odd ways. If talking back is a symptom of a strained relationship at home, then a little understanding and TLC can go a long way to smoothing things out.

CHAPTER 15

—◆◇◆—

Children Who Manipulate, Whine, and Lie

Children manipulate, whine, and lie because they are children. They want whatever feels good, and they view their parents as gatekeepers to all the pleasures in the world. When they are denied, they are often inspired to find a way to get what they want—whether it's a later bedtime, more dessert, or a video game. Children often make demand after demand, followed by begging and whining that often wears down even the strongest parent. It is up to parents to teach children that their tricks and games won't work in the long run.

How do children manipulate? Let me count the ways.

- They make parents feel guilty. ("If you helped me more with my math homework, I wouldn't have failed, and then you wouldn't be punishing me.") Remember, a guilty parent is a good candidate for turning into a wimpy parent.

- They intimidate their parents with their anger. A child having a full-blown temper tantrum can make an insecure parent feel he is being too strict or is hurting his child by saying no. Don't fall for that.
- Some kids manipulate by escalating the bad behavior. Often the more a child misbehaves, the better the chance that the parents will cave in.
- They threaten: "I hate you" or "I'm going to live with Daddy." It is amazing how effective threats like these can be. Some parents are so upset to think that their children could hate them, or so fearful of losing custody of their children, that they immediately try to calm them by giving in.
- They play sick. "Mommy, my stomach hurts." "Daddy, I don't feel well." Sometimes these complaints are true, but they may be exaggerated in order to win sympathy and favors.
- Children often say, "But all the other kids are doing it." (Translation: "Other mommies and daddies are good, but you are really mean.") This tactic makes parents feel out of step with the rest of the parenting world.
- Some kids are just too good to be true. Watch out for the kid who butters you up with compliments and favors just prior to making an unreasonable request.

The Whining Child

For some parents, whining is the equivalent of fingernails scraping across a chalkboard. It is so physically irritating that kids discover it's a great means of manipulation.

When a child whines by begging, nagging, and acting

pathetic all in one breath, many loving parents cave in. When the child gets a lot of attention while she is whining—her parent argues with her to persuade her to give up her demand, or is reduced to screaming—it just encourages her to continue whining.

If the parent gives in on occasion, then the whining may actually get worse. Psychologists understand that good behavior or bad behavior is strengthened by periodically offering a reward. In other words, by being inconsistent you are not weakening the habit of whining; you are actually making it stronger.

Staying In Charge

One day while your child is talking to you in a normal way, turn on a tape recorder and record about three to four minutes of this conversation. Keep the recorder close by, because you want to capture your child when he goes into his whining routine. This time you will be recording the whiner in action.

A parent should do this because most kids have no idea what you mean when you shout, "Stop that whining!" Little kids, who are the most likely to whine, do not understand what you are talking about.

Once you have your two recordings, get your child's attention by telling him you want him to listen to something. First, play the normal conversation. While you do this, comment on how this is his "big-boy voice" and how nice and grown-up he sounds. Then play the recording of his whining. As he listens to this, label this his "little-boy voice" and say that this is not the way for a boy his age to ask for things. State: "From now on, I will not talk to you when you whine. I will respond to you only when I hear your big-boy voice."

When you do this you have set the stage for a very powerful strategy: planned ignoring. This is when a parent purposefully decides to pretend his child is invisible, and offers no attention whatsoever while the child is involved in pesty behavior. You want to withdraw your attention during the whining and give your child attention the moment the whining stops. In this way you teach your child that a grown-up voice gives him a better chance of working things out with his parents.

If you don't want to bother using a recorder, you can accomplish the same goal by telling him in a nice and loving way how he sounds. Simply mimic him when he talks to you properly. Then show him what whining sounds like. The next time he whines you can say, "Now stop that, and talk to me in a big-boy voice." If your child ignores you, reinforce the message; "I will not talk to you until I hear a big-boy voice."

If you find that your child persists in whining, walk into another room. If your child follows you, ignore him or take him to his room for a time-out.

When he isn't whining while making a request, you can reward him by drawing his attention to his improvement. Simply say "I'm proud that you are asking for things in a grown-up way." There are many ways to praise your child. Don't take the new behavior you are experiencing for granted.

The Problem with Lying

It's not unusual for a child to lie to get his own way. Sometimes it takes parents days to discover they have been manipulated by a lie. Your son says, "I'm going to play at

Bobby's house." The truth is, he is going to play with Thomas, a boy you have forbidden him to see because he plays with matches.

Anyone who spends time with children knows that children can invent many different kinds of lies. Children lie to make people feel better, to break rules they don't agree with, to protect others, to gain approval, or to avoid an obligation. And, of course, children lie to con a friend or parent out of something.

How to Handle Lying

- Set a good example. You are training your children to lie when you have them tell Grandma that you're not home. (You are also being wimpy.)
- Try having two punishments when your child lies. One punishment for lying and one for the misdeed that is covered up.
- I like to teach children that when they lie, they need to make it up to the other person: "You did a wrong, now make it right."
- Point out that it is hard to always be honest.
- Reward children for being truthful. ("I appreciate that you told me you broke that dish.")
- Remove temptation for lying. Don't say, "Why did you do that?" Chances are the response will be a lie. Instead say, "What happened that you had to break the rule about doing homework?"

CHAPTER 16

Picky Eaters

When parents say they hate dinnertime, they almost always are living with a finicky or picky eater. This is the kid who starts gagging at the sight of your meal and gives out a lot of "yuk"s and "I'm not going to eat that stuff." These kids typically have a habit of looking sick or disgusted with whatever is being prepared.

This is pesty behavior because these children usually manage to dominate dinnertime. They are the center of attention as the parents vacillate between trying to persuade the child to eat and threatening the child. One minute it's "Please, sweetheart, try one more bite." And the next it's "You're not leaving this table until you have eaten everything on your plate."

While this is going on, the other kids who are eating are being ignored by parents who are giving 100 percent of their time to their obstinate child. The picky eater has two advantages with her stubbornness: she is getting lots of attention, and she is stealing attention from her siblings. (This can be a sibling rivalry problem in disguise.)

Understand that:

- Children do not eat more when they are forced to sit at the table.
- You can't make a child chew or swallow.

Managing the Picky Eater

Make eating your child's responsibility. It was your responsibility when he was a baby, but now it is your child's responsibility. You accomplish this by saying, "We have decided that whether you eat or not is up to you. I'll prepare your favorite meals a couple of times a week, but the rest of the time, you can choose from what is on the table." With this statement, you are putting an end to those awful power struggles. You are also dethroning the prince who has dominated family meals. In addition, you are setting the stage for your child to experience a logical consequence—hunger. When you don't eat, you get hungry.

Make sure that your child comes to the table hungry. Put a stop to snacking before mealtimes. Picky eaters have a habit of grazing on junk food all day long, so they have little motivation to enjoy a meal.

Limit dinnertime to just twenty minutes, or whatever you feel is reasonable to complete dinner. Use a kitchen timer so your child can hear the buzzer go off. When it does, remove his plate while announcing that dinner is over. Chances are he will have none of this. He will launch himself into an Academy Award–winning performance, announcing that he is starving and you are keeping him from eating. Don't give in.

Finally, let natural consequences teach your child that dinnertime is for eating. Later when your child resumes his dramatic acting and tries to convince you he is starving, do not make him a grilled cheese sandwich. Let him be hungry so he catches on that eating is his responsibility, not Mom's or Dad's.

Just remember, when your child accuses you of sending him to bed hungry, that you never denied him the opportunity to eat. If your child is hungry it is because he has chosen not to eat. If you feel guilt, you are recalling your own childhood, when you were sent to bed without dinner as punishment, but this is not the same thing. You served dinner, and it was your child's choice not to eat it.

Have the picky eater help prepare the menu for the week. When kids become involved with planning they are more cooperative at mealtimes, especially when they can include some of their favorite foods and dishes. Get your picky eater to help prepare the meals as well. When these kids start making dessert and mixing the salad, they are often more likely to eat the meal.

CHAPTER 17

❦

Morning Procrastinators

Imagine this scene: It is morning, and you have tried to get your child out of bed at least five times. Finally he is sitting on the edge of the bed and you are scolding him, urging him to hurry and get ready. You leave his bedroom to finish dressing and attend to other matters. When you return to your son's room you find that he has only one sock on. You yell and scream and start putting on his other sock and then his pants. At this point, after giving out more threats, you leave. A short time you come back to discover that he is playing with his Legos. Now you are brushing his teeth for him, looking for his backpack, and trying to serve him a decent breakfast. Finally, you get this rascal dressed, sort of fed, and at the bus stop on time. You are exhausted and it's all of eight o'clock in the morning. You are dealing with one of the most common and annoying pesty behaviors—that of the morning procrastinator.

Tomorrow you will repeat the same experience, because your child has not learned one thing from this craziness about being responsible. He hasn't learned, because he misbehaved this morning as he has every other morning in the past, and only you, the parent, have suffered the consequences. As we've seen, for poor behavior to change into appropriate behavior, the person doing the misbehaving has to experience some negative consequence. The parent in this situation suffers a negative consequence by having a miserable morning. The child ends up actually being rewarded by receiving attention, even though it is negative attention. If there are other children in the house, he has diverted Mom's or Dad's attention away from everyone else. He has managed to have someone else do all the work of getting him ready for school. And he may have had more time to play in the morning. Why should he change when everything is going his way?

When parents complain to me that they hate mornings, I'm fairly confident that they are living with a morning procrastinator. These are kids who might as well wear a sign around their necks that reads: "I'll go to school, but you will have to do all the work." They just will not take responsibility for getting themselves out of bed and ready for school.

The parents of one of these procrastinators has to overfunction and do for the child what the child should be doing for himself. At the same time the parent is dealing with other children and most likely getting herself ready for work. The parent feels frantic about the child's skipping breakfast and missing the school bus and is concerned that if the child arrives at school hungry, messy-looking, and late, it's the parent who will be blamed. The end result is that the parent feels blackmailed into doing all the work.

I have known parents who brush their children's teeth, comb their hair, pull on their socks, and so on.

Dealing with the Morning Procrastinator

Understand that it is not your job to get your child to school on time. Your job is to teach your child to take responsibility for getting herself ready for school.

Pick a moment in the day when you can sit down and have a heart-to-heart with the dawdler. Since you are going to end up criticizing her, I recommend that you start off by pointing out some of her strong points. (It is always best to build a kid up before tearing her down with a zing about how she is not behaving properly.) You might say something like: "You know how proud I am of you. You have many good friends, and you're a great speller, and your teachers say you behave well in school. But you know there is one area you have to work on." This is where you add the zing: "You're a big girl now, and it is time for you to get yourself ready for school. So beginning tomorrow there will be some new rules about the morning." And then inform your procrastinator how life will change.

Here are the rules:

- "I will set your alarm clock to wake you up. I will come into your room only two times to make sure you get out of bed to start getting ready."
- "If you are in the kitchen and dressed for school by seven fifteen then I will have time to make you breakfast." Use whatever time makes sense, and if necessary explain how to tell time or use a kitchen timer that is set to go off at 7:15.

- Continue, "If you are not dressed by seven fifteen I will not have time to get breakfast ready." Some children love breakfast, and this will matter to them. The important point is that she may miss breakfast if she is not ready on time. Parents often worry about their youngster being hungry on the bus. That's the idea! The logical consequence of running late is missing breakfast. Just give your child a multivitamin and an apple and remind yourself that this process will not go on forever.
- "If you are not dressed and ready to get on the school bus, I will put your clothes in a shopping bag and you will have to get dressed in school." If necessary, you may have to drive her to school—with the bag of clothes. If this will make you late to work, understand it will only last a few mornings. From my experience, if you end up driving your child to school, by the time you arrive at school your youngster will be diving for the shopping bag in the backseat to get herself dressed because she is embarrassed.

During the first morning confrontation, it is important for you to have the right attitude: You need to stay calm and resist nagging. You want to send the message to your child that this is her problem and not yours. She is the one who is going to be really unhappy with the consequences. As noted previously, children will never change their behavior as long as their misbehavior results in no penalties and only the parent has the bad time. Children change when their misbehavior is followed by a consequence that affects them.

CHAPTER 18

—◦◦◦—

School Problems

Every parent wants his child to be a success in school, but chances are good that your child, like all children, is going to get mixed reviews. Some of her behavior will be applauded; some will be criticized. No child grows up without making mistakes.

Some children, however, seem to be forever not settling down to what school is all about: they talk out of turn, they dawdle with their classwork, they get out of their seat when they feel like it. And they show little respect for the teacher's rules. (Far from being teacher's pet, they need to be tamed and trained.)

Some children have a hard time conforming. These children want everything to be on their own terms and have not been taught basic civilized behavior before they entered school. They may be without a host of skills like sharing, cooperating with others, respecting authority, tolerating frustration, and knowing right from wrong. Many of these kids have been raised at home as brats and enter the classroom as potential problems.

Efforts by teachers and parents seem to have little effect on these children. Often, the teacher sends notes home to the parents, essentially asking, "What are you going to do about this?" The parents in return get defensive and respond, "You're the teacher; can't you control your own class?" And the difficult student continues to get away with having a behavior problem in school while soaking up all kinds of attention.

The Note from the Teacher

Sooner or later your child will be criticized by a teacher. First, you want to take seriously any negative observations the school passes on to you. Most teachers are pretty good observers and are in a position to help parents see where the child is progressing and where he needs help. One of the first things you should do when a critical note arrives is to figure out if the criticism is justified. Whenever a teacher criticizes your child, watch out for your first instinct, which is to feel offended and to protect your child by criticizing the teacher. The teacher may be wrong, but more likely she is doing you a favor by bringing something to your attention.

School is more than reading, writing, and arithmetic. School represents your child's world away from home. The teacher is in a unique position to comment on a child's emotional and social development as well as his academic development. In school, your child is facing a number of challenges: He has to sit quietly for long periods of time. He has to raise his hand to ask for help. He has to cope with making mistakes. He must finish his work within certain time limits, and he must get along with his teacher, an authority figure. He has to make and keep friends and even deal with bullies. In other words, your child is working at becoming a self-disciplined person, which is why you want to take seriously the observations of your child's teacher.

Behavior Problems

There are many ways your child can misbehave in school. Sometimes children don't finish assignments. They bother their classmates; they speak out of turn and easily become silly. Typically children carry on like this because their behavior pays off. They avoid their work and also get a lot of negative attention. It's important for children to feel that there are daily consequences to their behavior at school.

The secret to correcting this situation is for the home and the school to connect and to work together as a team. As long as the school works independently of the parents and the parents are independent of the school, the acting-up child will fall through the educational cracks and continue his ways.

The bridge between home and school is a *behavior report card*. This type of report card for kids between kindergarten and sixth grade is one you make up and that the child takes to school every day. On this card are several of the problems this child has in school. At the end of the school day the teacher scores this behavior on the card. Behavior that is improving receives a plus sign and behavior that is not improving rates a minus sign. If a child returns home from school with not enough pluses, he loses a set number of privileges for that day. This works well because parents and school have joined forces so that the child is held accountable for poor behavior.

To set up a behavior report card, here are four typical behaviors you may list:

- Completes classroom assignments
- Follows class rules
- Cooperates with teacher
- Cooperates with classmates

You can easily have other categories, but these are four typical categories that have to be covered. At the end of the school day, the teacher will look over all four categories and assign a plus or minus. It is important for the teacher to look for relative improvement. "Has this child demonstrated some improvement today in this category?" As the weeks go by, the teacher should continue to ask this question while raising her standards. As the child improves, the teacher will expect more good behavior for the child to earn a plus.

At the end of the school day the parents review this card with their child. For the first week the child will need just two pluses to keep all privileges. The second week the child will need three pluses, and then the following week he needs four pluses to retain privileges.

Typical privileges are:

- going out to play after school
- having a friend over
- regular bedtime schedule
- making phone calls
- watching TV or videos
- playing computer games

Essentially, the child who doesn't score enough pluses ends

up going to bed earlier and not being allowed to watch TV or go out to play. If this sounds harsh, remember that you are trying to change behavior that has become entrenched. The goal is to make home unpleasant enough so that in school the child will think, "I'd better behave or I will have to go to bed early and can't go out and play." It is a good idea when you send your child off to school to say something like "I hope you have a terrific day so you can have all your privileges tonight."

Before you start using this strategy, you should sit down with your child; talk about how things are not going well in school and that you have a plan to help him do better. Then introduce the idea of the behavior report card.

Q: What if the report card is lost?

A: A lost report card is considered the same as a report card with all minuses. He will lose all privileges.

Q: What if the report card is left in school?

A: Again, your child loses privileges.

Q: What if my child writes in his own pluses?

A: Children have been known to forge pluses, so I advise teachers to initial each plus.

Q: What if my child is really upset over losing his privileges?

A: Good. That's exactly what you want. He has probably been driving his teachers crazy, and now he can't get away with it. He should be upset. You can say, "I know you feel bad that you lost privileges, but tomorrow is another day. You can have all your privileges back if you follow the rules." Remember that immature children need a lot of structure to improve their behavior, and the behavior report card provides that structure.

You stop using this method, with the teacher's consulta-tion, when you see real improvement. In time, new and more positive patterns of behavior are established. This report card plan works because it ties school and home together. The child usually does not regress. The newly found success at school is in itself rewarding, and both parent and teacher will continue to acknowledge his growth with periodic praise. Once new behaviors have been established, they don't need to be rewarded daily.

A FINAL WORD

—◦◦◦—

Whenever I give parenting talks, I always ask the audience to think about and share memories of their own parents. Inevitably what they recall are moments of fun and delight: I hear stories of picnics and amusement parks, Christmas mornings and birthday celebrations.

It's easy to forget that the purpose of having children is to enjoy them—to create special memories for them to cherish. I hope that by showing you how to be less wimpy, I have helped you put more joy back into your family.

Someday there will come a time when you will open the jelly jar and find only jelly. No bits of butter, no crumbs, no traces of peanut butter—just jelly. That's always the telltale sign that children no longer live in the house! So now is the time to really embrace your family.

Remember the story of how my three-year-old daughter, Connie, had a temper tantrum in the supermarket, and I had to carry her out of the store for a time-out? Well, that little girl is now thirty-four years old and far from a brat! She is a college graduate, owns a business, and has her own little daughter, Madison Mary. I watch with great pleasure and empathy as my daughter confidently manages her own daughter's temper tantrums. It is awesome to experience your child as an adult and then as a parent who practices what you preached to her about life. I wish you all the same awesome experience someday.

THOMAS GIETZEN

ABOUT THE AUTHORS

KENNETH N. CONDRELL, Ph.D., is a child psychologist and family counselor who has been helping children and families for over thirty years. He is the founder and director of the Condrell Center, a group practice of twenty-four psychologists specializing in counseling families, children, and teens. Dr. Condrell is an assistant clinical professor in the Department of Psychiatry, School of Medicine, at the State University of New York at Buffalo. Dr. Condrell has appeared on NBC's *Today* show, *Sally Jessy Raphaël*, and CNN's *Take Two*. He is seen weekly on NBC-TV's Buffalo, NY, station, and has his own call-in radio show, *Kid Talk*. He is the coauthor of *Be a Great Divorced Dad*.

LINDA LEE SMALL is the coauthor of *Be a Great Divorced Dad* and *A New Mother's Home Companion*, and is a contributing editor/writer for *The Women's Complete Healthbook*. A former contributing editor to *Ms*. magazine, her articles have been published in most of the national women's magazines, including *Parents*, *Women's Day*, *Redbook*, *Working Mother*, *McCalls*, *Self*, *Cosmopolitan*, *Child*, *Working Woman*, *Seventeen*, *Ladies' Home Journal*, and *Glamour*. She was appointed to the New York City Commission on the Status of Women. She lives in Brooklyn, New York, with her husband and her teenage son.